Marika Carboni

The Financial Impact of Political Connections

Industry-Level Regulation and the Revolving Door

palgrave
macmillan

Marika Carboni
Università degli Studi Roma Tre
Rome, Italy

ISBN 978-3-319-52775-8 ISBN 978-3-319-52776-5 (eBook)
DOI 10.1007/978-3-319-52776-5

Library of Congress Control Number: 2017936476

Cover image: Détail de la Tour Eiffel © nemesis2207/Fotolia.co.uk

Printed on acid-free paper

This Palgrave Macmillan imprint is published by Springer Nature
The registered company is Springer International Publishing AG
The registered company address is: Gewerbestrasse 11, 6330 Cham, Switzerland

Preface

This book is inspired by the interest toward the relationships between the economic and political worlds. Such links are assuming an increasing importance in the current atmosphere at the global level, and consequently they represent a highly topical subject.

Therefore, the book is dedicated to all readers who wish to deepen the understanding of such themes. Even though it is mainly addressed to specialists, it can also be approached by a nonspecialist audience. The current attention toward this topic may be able to both stimulate the debate and encourage further studies in this field.

Acknowledgments

There are a lot of people that I would like to thank. First, I truly wish to thank Franco Fiordelisi, my supervisor during the PhD program. Words are not enough to express my gratitude for everything he has done for me. He showed me the way and patiently led me step by step to achieve goals I did not believe possible to reach. He is always there to inspire, support, and mentor his students, both personally and professionally; this makes him the supervisor that I wish everyone had.

I would also like to convey my heartfelt gratitude to Alessandro Carretta, for his valuable advice and for having trusted and supported me along the way, enhancing my personal and professional growth. I am aware that I have been blessed to meet such great people in my life, and I thank God for that. I also wish to thank Anjan Thakor for having given me the opportunity to visit Olin Business School (Washington University in St. Louis) during the Spring Semester of the 2015–2016 academic year. I will always remember that extraordinary experience, and all the things that I have learnt from him and all the staff members, especially from Radha Gopalan, to whom I would also like to express my gratitude. I also truly wish to thank Ornella Ricci for her precious help, encouragement, and important suggestions, and Giovanni Cerulli for his teaching in the last year. Furthermore, I wish to thank Lucia Leonelli for her encouragement and support.

Moreover, I would like to thank Università degli Studi di Roma "Tor Vergata", Olin Business School (Washington University in St. Louis) and Università degli Studi Roma Tre, where I had the outstanding opportunity to design my models, collect data, run my empirical analysis and discuss my results. In addition, I want to thank Eleonora Carboni, Leopoldo Catania, Vincenzo D'Apice, Francesco Lannutti, Jacopo Raponi, Jorge Sabat, Francesco Saverio Stentella Lopes, my entire family, friends, peers, and professors for having been a part of my professional development and for helping me so much during my PhD studies. I will always remember both their support and all the interesting conversations we had in Rome, Naples, and St. Louis.

Last but not least, I am grateful to my parents, since they have been and are always there to support me. I also love them immensely.

Contents

List of Figures

List of Tables

CHAPTER 1

Introduction on Political Connections

Abstract This chapter introduces the topic of political connections. Specifically, it employs both anecdotal evidence and the reference to academic publications to show that political connections are assuming a growing importance and nowadays represent a very hot topic. On the basis of anecdotal evidence, the revolving door movement is assuming greater importance in the United States. With regard to academic publications, several studies focus on the measuring of the benefits of being politically connected, for example, in terms of performance. A group of papers shows the existence of a positive link between political connections and industry-level regulation. By relating to such a group, this book exhaustively investigates that link by selecting the most regulated industries in the United States. In addition, it investigates market reaction to the dates of announcement of new political connections. Unique results are guaranteed thanks to the use of a hand-collected dataset.

Keywords Anecdotal evidence · Revolving door movement · Political connections

This book focuses on political connections in the United States. Such a topic is assuming a growing importance, particularly in recent years. Especially after the financial crisis, the existence of a link between politics and firms is raising public opinion's interest. The great attention toward

M. Carboni, *The Financial Impact of Political Connections*,
DOI 10.1007/978-3-319-52776-5_1

the Goldman Sachs case may be emblematic in this sense. In 2008, *The New York Times* reports that: "Goldman's presence in the department and around the federal response to the financial crisis is so ubiquitous that other bankers and competitors have given the star-studded firm a new nickname: Government Sachs".[1] A few years later, *The Huffington Post* highlights that: "The close relationship between Wall Street and Washington belies their 200 mile separation".[2] According to the article, not only money but also people moved from Wall Street to Washington, and they were also moving in the opposite direction. Such a movement of people is commonly described by using the image of a revolving door, with people moving from business to politics and vice versa. This phenomenon is assuming greater importance in the United States. For example, according to *The Huffington Post*: "Chevron's lobbyists are a Who's Who of former government officials."[3] More generally, in 2010, *The Washington Post* reports that: "Three out of every four lobbyists who represent oil and gas companies previously worked in the federal government, a proportion that far exceeds the usual revolving-door standards on Capitol Hill".[4] Furthermore, in 2014, *The New York Times* reports that,[5] since 2007, over 1600 House or Senate staff members have registered to lobby in less than one year after they left the US Congress. As highlighted by an article published in 2015 in Bloomberg,[6] also the banking's revolving door is turning faster: in fact, the percentage of workers moving from regulatory jobs to banks (and vice versa) has increased since 1988.

Interestingly, while the habit of moving from public service into the private sector and vice versa is quite common in the United States, it seems to be a growing phenomenon in Europe. This is highlighted by the *Financial Times* in 2016: "News that Lord King, the former governor of the Bank of England, has taken a key advisory role at Citigroup follows only weeks after it was announced that former European Commission president José Manuel Barroso would chair Goldman Sachs International".[7]

In some cases, especially when the revolving door movement reaches a particular relevance, questions about a potential conflict of interests issue are raised. For example, the above-mentioned article published in *The New York Times* reports that outside executives and analysts observed that the decisions made at Treasury by Goldman alumni influenced the company's fortunes.[8] Yet another case of potential conflict of interest occurred when Carmen Segarra, a former New York Fed examiner, claimed that her colleagues were excessively respectful to Goldman Sachs.[9] Another example involves the Food and Drug Administration (FDA), and specifically concerns a slow response on the BMPEA (a chemical almost identical to amphetamine). As reported by *The New York Times* in 2015[10]: "Much of the responsibility for the F.D.A.'s sluggish response must fall on Dr. Daniel Fabricant",[11] who had left his job at the Natural Products Association (which is a group for supplement sellers and makers) to join the FDA's division of dietary supplement programs, and later returned as the chief executive of the trade group.

The greater importance reached by the revolving door trend and more generally by the political connections issue turns all the aforesaid examples into hot topics on a global level. This view is widely supported not only by anecdotal evidence but also by an increasing number of academic publications. Various studies measure the financial benefits of being politically connected by documenting abnormal returns (ARs) around specific events (for example, Faccio 2006; Goldman et al. 2009), and more generally, a large stream of research shows that political connections are associated with higher firms' value and performance (for example, Faccio 2006; Claessens et al. 2008; Ferguson and Voth 2008; Goldman et al. 2009; Bunkanwanicha and Wiwattanakantang 2009; Cooper et al. 2010; Kim et al. 2012; Ovtchinnikov and Pantaleoni 2012; Amore and Bennedsen 2013; Akey 2015). However, with respect to this link, results are conflicting, as a group of papers shows that politically connected firms underperform nonpolitically connected firms (Fan et al. 2007; Duchin and Sosyura 2012; Faccio et al. 2006).

Politically connected firms are also more likely to have access to federal investment funds (Duchin and Sosyura 2012), to be bailed-out by the government (Faccio et al. 2006), and to experience an increase in procurement contracts (Goldman et al. 2013). In addition, political connections are associated with preferential access to finance and larger loans (Claessens et al. 2008; Khwaja and Mian 2005) even if, unexpectedly, Bunkanwanicha and Wiwattanakatang (2009) show that politically connected companies do not borrow more.

Several papers investigate the relevance of political connections, finding that they are significant in countries characterized by high levels of corruption (Fisman 2001; Faccio 2006). However, more recent papers (for example, Goldman et al. 2009) argue that political connections are valuable also in strong legal environments. Such a finding represents the starting point of this book, as it focuses on the strong legal context of the United States.

A group of papers focusing on political connections shows that a positive link exists with industry-level regulation (for example, Bunkanwanicha and Wiwattanakatang 2009; Cooper et al. 2010). Regulation indeed plays a crucial role for firms, since it may be costly and may represent an impediment to business development. Therefore, companies in highly regulated industries should be more interested in being connected with politicians, as they could try to shape a better regulatory impact. This book links to the last group of papers. However, instead of focusing only on a limited number of highly regulated industries (for example, Bunkanwanicha and Wiwattanakatang 2009; Cooper et al. 2010), it exhaustively investigates whether highly regulated firms are more likely to be connected with politicians by selecting the 15 most regulated industries in the years between 1999 and 2014, within the strong legal and regulatory framework of the United States. Crucial is the use of RegData (Al-Ubaydli and McLaughlin 2015), which counts the words in the Code of Federal Regulations referring to a forbidden or required activity, and then ranks them based on the industries they probably affect (McLaughlin and Sherouse 2016). Moreover, thanks to a unique dataset going from 1999 to 2014, it is possible to investigate the link between industry-level regulation and political connections with respect to different years. Importantly, the long period of time allows to thoroughly study the market reaction to the dates of announcement of new political connections, in order to investigate the investors' evaluation of this matter. Specifically, this work innovates with regard to the consideration of industry-level regulation as a discriminating factor in the investigation of firm value creation.

The main findings are the following: (i) political connections are more likely to be established in companies operating in highly regulated industries, with regard to former politicians joining such firms; (ii) after controlling for firms' characteristics, political connections are more likely to be established across companies operating in highly regulated industries, regardless of the occurrence of a recession; (iii) the probability that a former politician, affiliated with the Republican Party, is either appointed as director or hired as corporate executive by a firm is higher in heavily regulated industries. Conversely, the same thing does not occur with respect to politicians affiliated with the Democratic Party; (iv) the probability that a former politician affiliated with the Republican Party is either appointed as director or hired as corporate executive by a firm is higher if the industry is highly regulated, if Republicans have the majority in the Congress, and the President is also Republican. Conversely, the probability that a former politician affiliated with the

Democratic Party is either appointed as director or hired as corporate executive by a firm is higher when the industry is not highly regulated, Democrats do not have the majority in the Congress, and the President is not a Democrat; and (v) there is significant evidence of a positive market reaction when a former politician joins a firm and if the latter either belongs to an industry subject to heavy regulation or is a top contractor. The results are consistent with the view that industry-level regulation matters.

This work contributes to two main strands of the literature: the first one studies the link between politics and business, and the second one investigates the impact of political connections on firm value. Nowadays, the presence and the relevance of politics in business, and vice versa, are widely accepted ideas, based on both anecdotal evidence and academic works. However, in spite of the growing body of this literature, to the author's knowledge, there is no study that directly focuses on industry-level regulation as a main determinant of political connections. Furthermore, this work contributes to the existing literature by employing a hand-collected dataset that allows to investigate the link between industry-level regulation and political connections, and by considering economic cycle and alternation of political powers. To the author's knowledge, industry-level regulation has not been thoroughly investigated heretofore, nor has it been considered as a crucial factor of the firm value creation.

This book is organized as follows. The second chapter reviews the relevant literature on political connections. The third chapter aims to investigate the link between industry-level regulation and political connections. It is also analyzed whether highly regulated firms are more likely to be politically connected during a recession. In the fourth chapter, relevance is given to political parties. Specifically, this chapter investigates whether firms operating in highly regulated industries are more likely to either hire as corporate executives or appoint as directors former politicians affiliated with either the Republican or the Democratic Party. In addition, this chapter investigates whether that probability increases depending on the "strength" of Republicans or Democrats in that moment. This research stems from the previous chapter's results. Specifically, it lays on the hypothesis that the interest of a firm to be politically connected is likely to be stronger if the industry is highly regulated. In addition, a firm should be particularly motivated to either hire or appoint a former politician affiliated with the Republican Party, relying on the belief that Republicans are generally thought of as being pro-business.[12] Furthermore, either hiring or appointing a former Republican should be more appealing for a firm if Republicans are in power, at that time. In the fifth chapter, an event study around the dates of announcement of former politicians joining firms and former directors, corporate executives, and founders entering politics is performed. Two subsamples are also considered. First, the top 100 contractors Report is used. Second, firms operating in highly regulated industries are taken into account. The expectation is that political connections add value, and therefore announcements should be associated with a positive cumulative abnormal return (CAR). In particular, market reaction to the announcement dates should be stronger for those firms subject to high regulation.

Notes

1. Julie Creswell and Ben White, "The Guys From 'Government Sachs'," *The New York Times*, October 17, (2008), accessed October 31, 2016, http://www.nytimes.com/2008/10/19/business/19gold.html.
2. Jillian Berman, "Wall Street and Washington Share Millions of Dollars, Lot of People," *The Huffington Post*, August 30, (2012), accessed October 31, 2016, http://www.huffingtonpost.com/2012/08/30/wall-street-washington_n_1842517.html.
3. Tyson Slocum, "Chevron Banks on Profitable Political Agenda," *The Huffington Post*, May 26, (2011), accessed October 31, 2016. http://www.huffingtonpost.com/tyson-slocum/chevron-banks-on-profitab_b_867408.html.
4. Dan Eggen and Kimberly Kindy, "Three of Every Four Oil and Gas Lobbyists Worked for Federal Government," *The Washington Post*, July 22, (2010), accessed October 31, 2016, http://www.washingtonpost.com/wp-dyn/content/article/2010/07/21/AR2010072106468.html.
5. Eric Lipton, "The Revolving Door: An Annotated Case Study," *The New York Times*, February 2, (2014), accessed October 31, 2016, http://www.nytimes.com/interactive/2014/02/02/us/politics/02revolving-door-documents.html.
6. Matthew Boesler and Jeff Kearns, "'Revolving Door' Between Fed and Banks Spins Faster," *Bloomberg*, January 30, (2015), accessed October 31, 2016, http://www.bloomberg.com/news/articles/2015-01-30/fed-s-revolving-door-spins-faster-as-banks-boost-hiring.
7. Patrick Jenkins, "'Revolving Door' Trend Takes Hold in Europe," *Financial Times*, July 29, (2016), accessed October 31, 2016, https://www.ft.com/content/4fc3a7b4-5599-11e6-9664-e0bdc13c3bef.
8. Julie Creswell and Ben White, "The Guys From 'Government Sachs'," *The New York Times*, October 17, (2008), accessed October 31, 2016, http://www.nytimes.com/2008/10/19/business/19gold.html.

9. Matthew Boesler and Jeff Kearns, "'Revolving Door' Between Fed and Banks Spins Faster," *Bloomberg*, January 30, (2015), accessed October 31, 2016, http://www.bloomberg.com/news/articles/2015-01-30/fed-s-revolving-door-spins-faster-as-banks-boost-hiring.
10. The Editorial Board, "Conflicts of Interest at the F.D.A.," *The New York Times*, April 13, (2015), accessed October 31, 2016, http://www.nytimes.com/2015/04/13/opinion/conflicts-of-interest-at-the-fda.html.
11. The Editorial Board, "Conflicts of Interest at the F.D.A.," *The New York Times*, April 13, (2015), accessed October 31, 2016, http://www.nytimes.com/2015/04/13/opinion/conflicts-of-interest-at-the-fda.html.
12. On this regard, see for example: "GOP Vs. Democrats: Who's Best For America's Economy?," *Forbes*, August 31, (2012), accessed October 31, 2016, http://www.forbes.com/sites/investopedia/2012/08/31/gop-vs-democrats-whos-best-for-americas-economy/#1dcce5a13e80.

CHAPTER 2

Literature Review on Political Connections

Abstract This chapter provides an in-depth analysis of the existing literature related to political connections. First, a classification of the different measures of political connection employed in previous works is provided. Second, the main findings of studies related to this topic are summarized, showing that political connections are valuable in different ways. More specifically, they are associated with higher firms' value and performance, preferential access to finance, and larger loans. Moreover, politically connected firms are more likely to be founded and bailed out. A group of papers shows a positive link between political connections and industry-level regulation. These studies generally refer to some highly regulated industries, while this book exhaustively investigates the link between political connections and industry-level regulation over 16 years (1999–2014) by selecting the most regulated industries in the United States. In addition, it investigates the market reaction to the dates of announcement of new political connections.

Keywords Measures of political connection · Industry-level regulation · Positive link

M. Carboni, *The Financial Impact of Political Connections*,
DOI 10.1007/978-3-319-52776-5_2

2.1 Introduction

The aim of this chapter is to provide a literature review of political connections. The definition of political connections is a primary issue to deal with for a paper related to such a topic, and thereby a review of the definitions employed in past studies along with a classification of the measures of political connections is provided. Subsequently, a summary of the main findings of papers on this topic is given with the aim of showing that political connections are valuable in several ways.

The remainder of this chapter is organized as follows. Section 2.2 provides a literature review on political connections and Section 2.3 concludes.

2.2 Literature Review

Different measures of political connections are used in the literature. By loosely following Ovtchinnikov and Pantaleoni (2012), it is possible to divide them in two main categories, namely "explicit" and "implicit" measures. The term "explicit measure" refers to the case of a current politician working in a firm and/or a current businessman entering politics. For example, Faccio (2006) defines a firm as politically connected if a firm's top officer or large shareholder is a member of parliament or a minister/the head of state. Khwaja and Mian (2005) identify a political company if its director runs for election, while Carretta et al. (2012) classify a bank as politically connected if a politician is sitting on the board of directors.

Conversely, the term "implicit measure" broadly refers to the following cases: (i) affiliations/documented friendships/family networks among firms and politics; (ii) political background of businessmen; (iii) firms' contributions to politics; (iv) firms' proximity to politics; (v) association between ownership and contribution; and (vi) lobbying activity. For example, Amore and Bennedsen (2013) take into account family networks. In Indonesia, Fisman (2001) considers firms that are connected to President Suharto's family. Specifically, he adopts the Suharto Dependency Index, namely a rating (from one to five) stating the degree of dependence for profitability on political connection of the largest industrial groups in Indonesia. For instance, firms linked to President Suharto's children obtain the highest score. Implicit political connections may also be identified by referring to the political background of directors (Goldman et al. 2009; Duchin and Sosyura 2012; Goldman et al. 2013).

In addition, even contributions either from businessmen or firms to Political Parties and Committees (for example, Ferguson and Voth 2008) should be included within implicit connections. By using data from the Center of Responsive Politics (CRP), Goldman et al. (2009) consider all the money donations made by companies to the Republican and Democratic Parties prior to the 2000 election in addition to the political background of directors and in order to identify political connections. Alternatively, Kim et al. (2012) employ the companies' proximity to political power through the development of a Political Alignment Index (PAI). Finally, Tahoun (2014) elaborates an original measure of political connection, which is referred to the association between ownership and contribution. Specifically, such a measure implies an association between share ownership by politicians and the contributions that companies give to their election campaigns. As Tahoun (2014) highlights, the ownership-contribution association represents a novel measure, as it defines the dimension in which politicians and companies mutually take care of each other. A further way by which firms try to affect government decisions is that of the lobbying activity. Interestingly, such activity correlates with companies' campaign contributions, implying that companies coordinate their actions to establish political networks (Akey 2015). With respect to this measure, Blanes I Vidal et al. (2012) demonstrate that lobbyists linked to US senators undergo an average 24% decline in generated revenue when senators leave office. In a more recent research, Borisov et al. (2015) find that companies characterized by high lobbying activity show a significant decrease in market value with respect to an event potentially able to limit their lobbying capacity. As they highlight, the decrease in firm value associated with lobbying expenditures in reaction to such an event supports the opinion that lobbying generates value for the shareholders. Finally, Duchin and Sosyura (2012) introduce four measures of political connection. Among them, they employ the amount of company's spending on lobbying banking regulators and the US Congress in the biennium 2008–2009.

Papers focusing on political connections demonstrate that they are valuable in different ways. In particular, a large stream of research shows that political connections are associated with higher firms' value and performance. For example, Faccio (2006) documents a strong increase in firm value at the announcement that a businessperson enters politics (but not even when a politician joins a firm). In particular, market reaction is larger when a businessperson becomes prime minister or a large shareholder is entering politics. By taking into account the 1998 and 2002 elections, Claessens et al. (2008) find that companies giving contributions to elected federal deputies show higher stock returns than others. Goldman et al. (2009) find that S&P 500 components with a Republican board outperform S&P 500 components with a Democratic board, following the presidential election held on November 7, 2000 (when the Republican Party won the elections). They also find positive ARs for appointments in firms of politically connected individuals, therefore showing that the establishment of a connection results in an increase of firm value. Symmetrically, a previous paper (Fisman 2001) finds that the end of a connection results in a decline of firm value: companies connected to the Suharto family lose indeed value at the announcements regarding the worsening health of President Suharto. Ferguson and Voth (2008) demonstrate that companies supporting the Nazis outperform other companies up to 8% over the period January–March 1933. In Thailand, Bunkanwanicha and Wiwattanakantang (2009) find that the more business owners trust concessions by the government or the richer they are, the more probable they are to run for election, and that the market value of their companies increases strongly once they are in politics. Cooper et al. (2010) show a positive association between political contributions and the operating performance of companies, while Kim et al. (2012) find that companies situated in high PAI states outperform companies situated in low PAI states. Ovtchinnikov and Pantaleoni (2012) provide evidence that political contributions are valuable when they are made not only by firms but also by individuals. In addition, Amore and Bennedsen (2013) find that an increase in political power improves the performance of politically connected companies.

In contrast to this large stream of research, a group of papers shows that political connections are associated to lower performance. In particular, Fan et al. (2007) find that companies having politically connected CEOs underperform other companies by nearly 18% in terms of stock returns (three-years after the Initial Public Offering). Duchin and Sosyura (2012) show that politically connected beneficiaries of government funds underperform unconnected beneficiaries. Faccio et al. (2006) find that the bailed-out companies that are politically connected show worse performance than the unconnected ones after and at the time of the bailout.

Politically connected firms are also more likely to be founded and bailed out. Duchin and Sosyura (2012) find a positive relation between political connections and companies' access to federal investment funds. In particular, after showing that much of public companies entitled to participate in Capital Purchase Program (CPP)[1] submitted applications, they demonstrate that political connections were positively associated with the probability of approval. In addition, Faccio et al. (2006) show that politically connected companies are more likely to obtain government funds in case of distress, in particular when those countries obtain funding from the World Bank or the International Monetary Fund. Moreover, Goldman et al. (2013) show that political connections are associated to a large increase of firms' procurement contracts. Firms connected to the winning party show indeed a rise in procurement contracts following the 1994 election, when a shift in political power from Democrats to Republicans occurred in both the House of Representatives and the Senate.

Political connections are also associated to preferential access to finance and larger loans. Specifically, Claessens et al. (2008) find that companies' campaign contributions positively influence their access to finance, as shown by the increase in bank leverage after an election. For Pakistan, Khwaja and Mian (2005) find that politically connected companies receive a favorable treatment in terms of loans. They obtain 45% larger loans, with 50% higher default rates on such loans. Such a special treatment refers to loans from government banks. However, despite the results provided by past papers, Bunkanwanicha and Wiwattanakatang (2009) do not document any benefit related to political power on corporate debt financing.

Past papers point out that political connections are relevant in countries with high levels of corruption (Fisman 2001; Faccio 2006). Nevertheless, more recent papers demonstrate that political connections are valuable also in strong legal environments. For example, Goldman et al. (2009) show that political connections have an impact on firm value even within a strong legal context such as the one of the United States. By considering the stock ownership by the members of the Congress of the United States, Tahoun (2014) shows that companies having a stronger association between ownership and contribution obtain more government contracts. Amore and Bennedsen (2013) show that connections are relevant also in Denmark, which is one of the less corrupt countries in the world. Specifically, the authors establish the causal effect of variations in political power, due to the enlargement of local governments after the 2005 administrative reform (which reduced the number of municipalities), on the performance of politically connected firms.

A group of papers highlights the existence of a positive link between political connections and industry-level regulation (for example,

Bunkanwanicha and Wiwattanakantang, 2009; Cooper et al. 2010). Generally, this group takes into account only a few highly regulated industries. Moreover, it does not seem to consider industry-level regulation as a crucial determinant of political connections. Conversely, by using RegData (Al-Ubaydli and McLaughlin 2015) and a unique dataset, it is possible to identify the most regulated industries of the Unites States, and exhaustively investigate the link between political connections and industry-level regulation over 16 years. In addition, this book analyzes market reaction to the dates of announcement of new political connections.

2.3 Conclusions

This chapter provides a literature review of political connections. First, different definitions used in past papers are reviewed by distinguishing between explicit and implicit measures. A summary of these measures is provided in Table 2.1. Second, the main findings of these papers are

Table 2.1 Measures of political connections in past papers

Authors and year	*Type of measure*
Akey (2015)	Implicit measure
Amore and Bennedsen (2013)	Explicit measure + implicit measure
Blanes I Vidal et al. (2012)	Implicit measure
Borisov et al. (2015)	Implicit measure
Bunkanwanicha and Wiwattanakatang (2009)	Explicit measure
Carretta et al. (2012)	Explicit measure
Claessens et al. (2008)	Implicit measure
Cooper et al. (2010)	Implicit measure
Duchin and Sosyura (2012)	Explicit measure + implicit measure
Faccio (2006)	Explicit measure + implicit measure
Faccio et al. (2006)	Explicit measure + implicit measure
Fan et al. (2007)	Explicit measure + implicit measure
Ferguson and Voth (2008)	Implicit measure
Fisman (2001)	Implicit measure
Goldman et al. (2009)	Implicit measure
Goldman et al. (2013)	Implicit measure
Khwaja and Mian (2005)	Explicit measure
Kim et al. (2012)	Implicit measure
Ovtchinnikov and Pantaleoni (2012)	Implicit measure
Tahoun (2014)	Implicit measure

summarized, showing that political connections are valuable in different ways. With respect to the place in which political connections are relevant, previous papers identify corrupt countries. However, a more recent strand of literature shows that political connections are relevant also in the United States and Denmark, namely in strong legal systems and low-corruption environments. Lastly, a further group of papers documents a positive association between political connections and industry-level regulation. This book relates to this group, but it investigates the link between political connections and regulation by exhaustively considering the most regulated industries in the United States over a period of time going from 1999 to 2014. Such a long period of time allows to thoroughly examine market reaction to the dates of announcement of new political connections, in order to investigate the investors' evaluation of this matter.

Note

1. As highlighted by Duchin and Sosyura (2012), the CPP is the first Troubled Asset Relief Program (TARP) initiative.

CHAPTER 3

Political Connections and Industry-Level Regulation

Abstract Industry-level regulation is a main concern for firms. Normally, companies oppose regulation, since they view it as costly and an impediment to business activities. Hence, firms in highly regulated industries should be more interested in being connected with politicians. By exploiting a unique database, this chapter investigates whether listed firms of the most regulated industries in the United States are more likely to be politically connected. Furthermore, it investigates whether listed firms of the most regulated industries are more likely to be politically connected when a recession occurs. To the author's knowledge, no studies exhaustively investigate the probability of a firm to be politically connected depending on its industry-level regulation. Furthermore, the long period of time (1999–2014) allows to take into account recessions, and hence analyze if this probability changes depending on the phases of economic cycles. The results show that industry-level regulation matters in establishing political connections.

Keywords Political connections · Highly regulated industries · Recession

3.1 Introduction

Industry-level regulation is crucial across firms. Generally, they oppose regulation, as it is considered expensive and an impediment to business activities. For this reason, firms in highly regulated industries should be

M. Carboni, *The Financial Impact of Political Connections*,
DOI 10.1007/978-3-319-52776-5_3

more interested in being connected with politicians. By exploiting a hand-collected database on political connections for the period 1999–2014, this chapter investigates whether listed firms in the most regulated industries in the United States are more likely to be politically connected (first research question). In addition, this chapter investigates whether listed firms in the most regulated industries are more likely to be politically connected when a recession occurs (second research question). The results show that the probability to be politically connected is higher for firms in the most regulated industries (but only by considering former politicians joining firms). Moreover, such a probability is higher for firms in the most regulated industries, regardless of the occurrence of a recession.

To the author's knowledge, no previous studies exhaustively investigate the probability of a firm to be politically connected depending on its industry-level regulation. Central in this study is the use of RegData (Al-Ubaydli and McLaughlin 2015). The RegData methodology gives a profound insight into the complexity of the regulatory documents as it properly focuses on the words expressing an obligation to comply with (Al-Ubaydli and McLaughlin 2015; McLaughlin and Sherouse 2016). Furthermore, the long period of time (1999–2014) allows to take into account recessions, and hence to analyze the probability of a firm to be politically connected depending on the phases of the economic cycle.

The remainder of this chapter is organized as follows. Section 3.2 provides the author's definition of political connection and describes the sample; Section 3.3 presents the methodology and the variables; Section 3.4 provides the results; and Section 3.5 concludes.

3.2 Definition of Political Connections and Sample

The definition of political connection considers the movement of both sides of a "revolving door", namely from business to politics and vice versa. The period of time considered is 2000–2014. In particular, a political connection exists when: (i) former directors, corporate executives, and founders[1] enter politics and (ii) former politicians, selected because in office over the period 2000–2014, join firms either as directors or as corporate executives.

Politicians are related to both the US Legislative (the Senate and the House of Representatives) and Executive Branches (specifically: the President, the Vice President, the principal executives of the Executive Office of the President, and the Cabinet[2]), and they are in office between January 2000 and September 2014. To collect the names of politicians, websites such as the Biographical Directory of the United States Congress, The White House, and OpenCongress are used. In the starting sample, the number of person-position combinations is 1,507. By using public data (available on websites such as Bloomberg, Reuters, and Forbes), politicians with a "business career" as directors, corporate executives, and/or founders, before or after entering politics, are identified. The focus is on listed firms, which are identified as "politically connected" if linked to a politician.

To associate a code to every firm, the Securities and Exchange Commission (SEC)'s EDGAR database is used. Therefore, politically connected firms are associated with the Central Index Key (CIK).[3] By analyzing filings provided by that database, it is possible to check and further identify both former politicians who join boards and directors who leave the board to enter politics. Lastly, an extensive keyword search on LexisNexis is performed in order to collect dates of announcement of corporate and political appointments and resignations.

With respect to politically connected firms, data are collected from CRSP and COMPUSTAT databases. In addition, data for S&P 500 components are gathered. A part of the firms in the Index is not politically connected (373 firms), while the rest is politically connected (101 firms). Furthermore, there are politically connected firms which are not in the Index (126). The sample also contains a third group of companies, which are neither S&P 500 components nor politically connected firms. Basically, those companies are in the dataset because they have the same Ticker symbols of either politically connected firms or S&P 500 components.[4] The final sample is described in Table 3.1. Further information and details on the dataset are available in Appendix A.

Table 3.1 Sample

S&P 500 Components (not Pcf)*	*Pcf (not S&P 500 Components)*	*S&P 500 Components and Pcf*	*Other (not Pcf)*	*Tot. number of listed firms*
373 (a)	126 (b)	101 (c)	19 (d)	619 (a + b + c + d)**

*"Pcf" stands for "politically connected firms".

**Nine firms are excluded from the sample since the construction of the control variables is not possible for them.

Source: Author's own

3.3 Methodology and Variables

A cross-sectional probit model is used to investigate whether firms in highly regulated industries are more likely to be politically connected, and therefore to answer the first research question. An interaction variable is then created by considering industry-level regulation and recession times, and a pooled probit model is used to investigate whether political connections are more likely to be established when firms are subject to high regulation and a recession occurs, and therefore to answer the second research question. The variables used in the model are defined as follows:

atleastonetimeconnected is a dummy variable taking value 1 if a firm is politically connected at least one time over the interval 1999–2014 (both sides of the revolving door), and 0 otherwise.

atleast_infirm is a dummy variable taking value 1 if a former politician, selected because in office over the time period January 2000–September 2014, joins a listed firm (as director or corporate executive) at least one time over the interval 1999–2014, and 0 otherwise.

atleast_inpolitics is a dummy variable taking value 1 if a former businessman, that was a founder or worked (as director or corporate executive) for at least one listed firm during his/her career, enters politics at least once over the time period January 2000–September 2014, and 0 otherwise.

atleastonetimeconnected, *atleast_infirm* and *atleast_inpolitics* are used as dependent variables in the cross-sectional probit regressions in order to answer the first research question.

bothsides is a dummy variable taking value 1 during the days in which a listed firm is politically connected (from the date of the announcement, or from the first available date), by considering both sides of the revolving door, and 0 otherwise.

infirm is a dummy variable taking value 1 during the days in which a former politician, selected because in office over the period January 2000–September 2014, works (as director or corporate executive) for a listed firm (from the date of the announcement, or from the first available date), and 0 otherwise.

inpolitics is a dummy variable taking value 1 during the days in which a former businessman, who was a founder or worked (as director or corporate executive) for at least one listed firm, is a politician in office over the period January 2000–September 2014 (from the date of the announcement, or from the first available date), and 0 otherwise.

bothsides, infirm, and *inpolitics* are used as dependent variables in the pooled probit regressions, in order to answer the second research question.

topregulatedind is a dummy variable taking value 1 if the industry is highly regulated, and 0 otherwise. The 15 most regulated industries for every year, going from 1999 to 2014, are selected by using RegData. By 3 digit-naics, they are: Chemical Manufacturing (325); Professional, Scientific, and Technical Services (541); Utilities (221); Transportation Equipment Manufacturing (336); Food Manufacturing (311); Support Activities for Transportation (488); Securities, Commodity Contracts, and Other Financial Investments and Related Activities (523); Petroleum and Coal Products Manufacturing (324); Credit Intermediation and Related Activities (522); Air Transportation (481); Animal Production (112); Oil and Gas Extraction (211); Water Transportation (483); Ambulatory Health Care Services (621); Telecommunications (517); and Fishing, Hunting, and Trapping (114). Data on financial statements from financial firms and utilities are different from others, and thereby not properly comparable to those of companies operating in other industries. Consequently, financial firms and utilities are excluded from the regressions when controls for firms' characteristics are added. Furthermore, nonoperating establishments are excluded too.

recession is a dummy variable taking value 1 during a recession (March 2001–November 2001 and December 2007–June 2009, according to The National Bureau of Economic Research - NBER: www.nber.org), and 0 otherwise. This variable is used in order to investigate if political connections are more likely to be established depending on the industry-level regulation and the occurrence of a recession (in order to answer the second research question).

Leverage2. Following Gorodnichenko and Weber (2016), leverage is computed as the ratio of long-term debt and debt in current liabilities to stockholders' equity, long-term debt, and debt in current liabilities. Leverage is an annual data, and it is lagged in the model. In particular, it is aligned with the data observable by the investors.[5] *Leverage2* is leverage after the winsorization at 1 and 99 percentile levels.

Roa2. Roa is the ratio between pretax income and total assets. It is an annual data, and it is lagged in the model. In particular, it is aligned with the data observable by the investors. *Roa2* is Roa after the winsorization at 1 and 99 percentile levels.

Size. *Size* is the natural log of total assets. It is an annual data, and it is lagged in the model. In particular, it is aligned with the data observable by the investors.

CIncR2. CIncR is the ratio between cost of goods sold and sales/turnover (net). It is an annual data, and it is lagged in the model. In particular, it is aligned with the data observable by the investors. *CIncR2* is CIncR after the winsorization at 1 and 99 percentile levels.

Table 3.2 summarizes the variables along with a description of each variable used in the analysis.

Table 3.2 List and definition of variables

Variable	*Variable definition*
atleastonetimeconnected	A dummy variable taking value 1 if a firm is politically connected at least once over the time interval 1999–2014 (both sides of the revolving door), and 0 otherwise.
atleast_infirm	A dummy variable taking value 1 if a former politician, selected because in office over the time period January 2000–September 2014, joins a listed firm (as director or corporate executive) at least once over the interval 1999–2014, and 0 otherwise.
atleast_inpolitics	A dummy variable taking value 1 if a former businessman, that was a founder or worked (as director or corporate executive) for at least one listed firm during his/her career, enters politics at least once over the time period January 2000–September 2014, and 0 otherwise.
bothsides	A dummy variable taking value 1 during the days in which a listed firm is politically connected (from the date of the announcement, or from the first available date), by considering both sides of the revolving door, and 0 otherwise.
infirm	A dummy variable taking value 1 during the days in which a former politician, selected because in office over the period January 2000–September 2014, works (as director or corporate executive) for a listed firm (from the date of the announcement, or from the first available date), and 0 otherwise.
inpolitics	A dummy variable taking value 1 during the days in which a former businessman, who was a founder or worked (as director or corporate executive) for at least one listed firm, is a politician in office over the period January 2000–September 2014 (from the date of the announcement, or from the first available date), and 0 otherwise.
topregulatedind	A dummy variable taking value 1 if the industry is heavily regulated, and 0 otherwise. By using RegData, the 15 most regulated industries for every year, going from 1999 to 2014, have been selected. By 3 digit-naics, the most regulated industries are:

Table 3.2 (continued)

Variable	*Variable definition*
	Chemical Manufacturing (325), Professional, Scientific, and Technical Services (541); Utilities (221); Transportation Equipment Manufacturing (336); Food Manufacturing (311); Support Activities for Transportation (488); Securities, Commodity Contracts, and Other Financial Investments and Related Activities (523); Petroleum and Coal Products Manufacturing (324); Credit Intermediation and Related Activities (522); Air Transportation (481); Animal Production (112); Oil and Gas Extraction (211); Water Transportation (483), Ambulatory Health Care Services (621); Telecommunications (517); Fishing, Hunting, and Trapping (114).
Recession	A dummy variable taking value 1 during a recession (March 2001–November 2001 and December 2007–June 2009, according to The National Bureau of Economic Research – NBER), and 0 otherwise.
Leverage2	Leverage is the ratio of long-term debt and debt in current liabilities to stockholders' equity, long-term debt, and debt in current liabilities. Leverage is an annual data, and it is lagged in the model. In particular, it is aligned with the data observable by the investors. *Leverage2* is leverage after the winsorization at 1 and 99 percentile levels.
Roa2	Roa is the ratio between pretax income and total assets. It is an annual data, and it is lagged in the model. In particular, it is aligned with the data observable by the investors. *Roa2* is Roa after the winsorization at 1 and 99 percentile levels.
Size	*Size* is the natural log of total assets. It is an annual data, and it is lagged in the model. In particular, it is aligned with the data observable by the investors.
CIncR2	CIncR is the ratio between cost of goods sold and sales/ turnover (net). It is an annual data, and it is lagged in the model. In particular, it is aligned with the data observable by the investors. *CIncR2* is CIncR after the winsorization at 1 and 99 percentile levels.

Source: Author's own

3.4 Results

Tables 3.3, 3.4, and 3.5 show the results of the cross-sectional probit regressions relating the probability of a firm to be politically connected to its belonging to a highly regulated industry. The coefficient of *topregulatedind* is positive and significant at 1% level, suggesting that the likelihood of firms to be politically connected is associated with belonging to a top regulated industry (Table 3.3). When the two sides of the revolving door are considered separately, the coefficient of *topregulatedind* remains positive and significant at 1% level if the dependent variable is *atleast_infirm*, suggesting that the likelihood of firms to either hire or appoint a former politician is associated with belonging to a top regulated industry (Table 3.4). The coefficient of *topregulatedind* is positive, but not

Table 3.3 Cross-sectional probit model, both sides of the revolving door

Dependent variable: atleastonetimeconnected	*Coef.*
1.*topregulatedind*	0.325^{***}
	(0.104)
_cons	-0.483^{***}
	(0.069)
N	619

$^{*}p < 0.1$; $^{**}p < 0.05$; $^{***}p < 0.01$; Robust standard errors in parentheses

Table 3.4 Cross-sectional probit model, former politicians in firm

Dependent variable: atleast_infirm	*Coef.*
1.*topregulatedind*	0.303^{***}
	(0.108)
_cons	-0.719^{***}
	(0.073)
N	619

$^{*}p < 0.1$; $^{**}p < 0.05$; $^{***}p < 0.01$; Robust standard errors in parentheses

significant at 10% level or less, if the dependent variable is *atleast_inpolitics* (Table 3.5).

Tables 3.6 and 3.7 show the average adjusted predictions (also known as "predictive margins"), as the sign of the coefficient only provides the direction of the effect. By considering both sides of the revolving door, the results suggest that for a firm, the probability to be politically connected (at least one time during the period 1999–2014) is equal to 43.7% if the industry is highly regulated, and equal to 31.5% if the industry is not highly regulated (Table 3.6). When the sample is divided, the probability to either hire or appoint a former politician is equal to 33.8% if the industry is highly regulated, and equal to 23.6% if the industry is not highly regulated (Table 3.7). Tables 3.8 and 3.9 summarize the relative average marginal effects. Specifically, the results show that the probability to be politically

Table 3.5 Cross-sectional probit model, former businessmen in politics

Dependent variable: atleast_inpolitics	*Coef.*
1.*topregulatedind*	0.144
	(0.128)
_cons	-1.171^{***}
	(0.086)
N	619

$^{*}p < 0.1$; $^{**}p < 0.05$; $^{***}p < 0.01$; Robust standard errors in parentheses

Table 3.6 Average adjusted predictions, both sides of the revolving door

Variables	*Average adjusted predictions*
0bn.*topregulatedind*	0.315^{***}
	(0.025)
1.*topregulatedind*	0.437^{***}
	(0.031)
N	619

$^{*}p < 0.1$; $^{**}p < 0.05$; $^{***}p < 0.01$

Table 3.7 Average adjusted predictions, former politicians in firm

Variables	*Average adjusted predictions*
0bn.*topregulatedind*	0.236***
	(0.023)
1.*topregulatedind*	0.338***
	(0.029)
N	619

*$p < 0.1$; **$p < 0.05$; ***$p < 0.01$

Table 3.8 Average marginal effects, both sides of the revolving door

Variables	*Average marginal effects*
1.*topregulatedind*	0.123***
	(0.039)
N	619

*$p < 0.1$; **$p < 0.05$; ***$p < 0.01$

Table 3.9 Average marginal effects, former politicians in firm

Variables	*Average marginal effects*
1.*topregulatedind*	0.102***
	(0.037)
N	619

*$p < 0.1$; **$p < 0.05$; ***$p < 0.01$

connected is 12.3% higher for a firm belonging to a top regulated industry with respect to a firm that does not, by considering both sides of the revolving door (Table 3.8). Moreover, the probability to either hire or appoint a former politician is 10.2% higher for a firm that belongs to a top regulated industry with respect to a firm that does not (Table 3.9). The percentages are equal to the difference between the average adjusted predictions.

The above results show that firms operating in the most regulated industries are more likely to be politically connected, disregarding the specific time period in which they are politically connected. The aim is now to investigate whether political connections are more likely to be established depending not only on the industry-level regulation but also on the phases of the economic cycle. In particular, the aim is to investigate if heavily regulated firms are more likely to be politically connected during a recession. Therefore, an interaction variable between ***topregulatedind*** and ***recession*** is created. The dependent variables (***bothsides***, ***infirm***, and ***inpolitics***) are constructed on a daily basis; specifically, they are dummy variables taking value 1 during the days in which a listed firm is politically connected. Table 3.10 shows the results of the pooled probit regression, first by considering both sides of the revolving door. The results show that companies are more likely to be politically connected if they belong to a highly regulated industry and a recession occurs (first column). The pooled probit regression is rerun by controlling for firms' characteristics, with the exclusion of financial firms, utilities, and nonoperating establishments. The results show that companies are more likely to be politically connected if

Table 3.10 Pooled probit model, both sides of the revolving door

Dependent variable: bothsides	*Coef.*	*Coef.*
0b.*topregulatedind*#1.*recession*	−0.027***	−0.042***
	(0.004)	(0.005)
1.*topregulatedind*#0b.*recession*	0.114***	0.190***
	(0.002)	(0.003)
1.*topregulatedind*#1.*recession*	0.119***	0.160***
	(0.005)	(0.006)
Leverage2		−0.008
		(0.006)
Roa2		−0.774***
		(0.012)
Size		0.035***
		(0.001)
CIncR2		0.095***
		(0.006)
_cons	−1.169***	−1.417***
	(0.002)	(0.008)
N	2,135,437	1,428,624

$^{*}p < 0.1$; $^{**}p < 0.05$; $^{***}p < 0.01$; Robust standard errors in parentheses

they belong to a highly regulated industry and a recession does not occur (second column). Table 3.11 shows the average adjusted predictions. After controlling for firms' characteristics (second column), the probability goes from a minimum of 12.1% (when a firm does not belong to a top regulated industry and a recession occurs) to a maximum of 17.4% (when a firm belongs to a top regulated industry and a recession does not occur). Figure 3.1 shows the predictive margins with respect to the last case.

The analysis is repeated by considering the two sides of the revolving door separately. In particular, when the movement from politics to firms is considered (Table 3.12), the results show that companies are more likely to be politically connected if they belong to a highly regulated industry and a recession does not occur (first column). The effect is nearly unchanged when controls for firms' characteristics are added (second column). The average adjusted predictions are showed in Table 3.13. After controlling for firms' characteristics (second column), the probability for a firm to be politically connected goes from a minimum of 8.4% (when a firm does not belong to a top regulated industry and a recession occurs) to a maximum of 12.3% (when a firm belongs to a top regulated industry and a recession does not occur). Figure 3.2 shows the predictive margins with respect to the last case.

By considering the movement from firms to politics (Table 3.14), the results show that companies are more likely to be politically connected if they belong to a highly regulated industry and in recession times (first column).

Table 3.11 Average adjusted predictions, both sides of the revolving door

Variables	*Average adjusted predictions*	*Average adjusted predictions*
0bn.*topregulatedind*#0bn.*recession*	0.121***	0.130***
	(0.000)	(0.000)
0bn.*topregulatedind*#1.*recession*	0.116***	0.121***
	(0.001)	(0.001)
1.*topregulatedind*#0bn.*recession*	0.146***	0.174***
	(0.000)	(0.001)
1.*topregulatedind*#1.*recession*	0.147***	0.167***
	(0.001)	(0.001)
N	2,135,437	1,428,624

*$p < 0.1$; **$p < 0.05$; ***$p < 0.01$

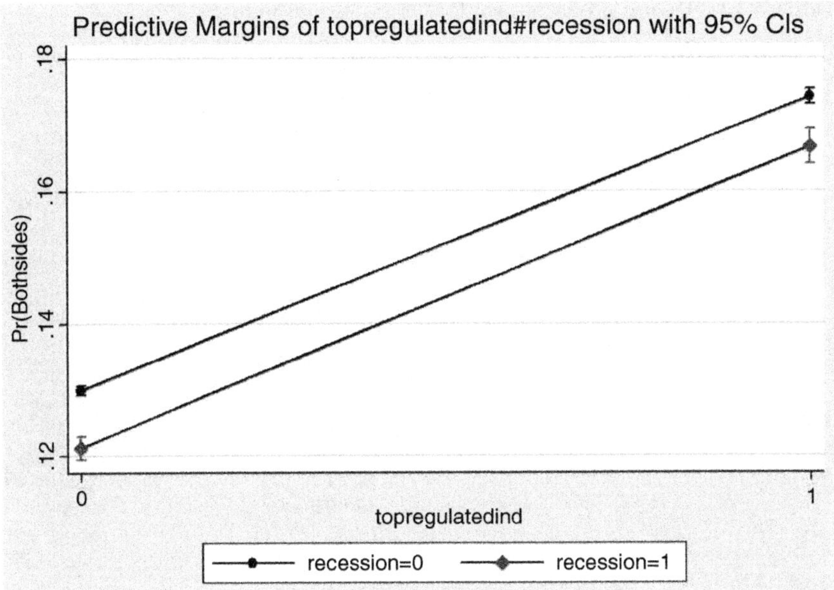

Fig. 3.1 Predictive margins, both sides of the revolving door

However, after controlling for firms' characteristics (second column), the results show that companies are more likely to be politically connected if they belong to a highly regulated industry and a recession does not occur. Table 3.15 shows the average adjusted predictions. After controlling for firms' characteristics (second column), the probability for a firm to be politically connected goes from a minimum of 3.5% (when a firm does not belong to a top regulated industry and a recession does not occur) to a maximum of 5.4% (when a firm belongs to a top regulated industry and a recession does not occur). Figure 3.3 shows the predictive margins with respect to the last case.

3.5 Conclusions

In this chapter, it is asked whether firms in heavily regulated industries are more likely to be politically connected and then whether they are more likely to be politically connected during recession times. To answer these questions, a unique, hand-collected database, which identifies all the

Table 3.12 Pooled probit model, former politicians in firm

Dependent variable: infirm	*Coef.*	*Coef.*
0b.*topregulatedind*#1.*recession*	-0.062***	-0.084***
	(0.005)	(0.005)
1.*topregulatedind*#0b.*recession*	0.069***	0.135***
	(0.003)	(0.003)
1.*topregulatedind*#1.*recession*	0.063***	0.120***
	(0.005)	(0.006)
Leverage2		-0.099***
		(0.006)
Roa2		-0.809***
		(0.013)
Size		0.035***
		(0.001)
CIncR2		0.049***
		(0.006)
_cons	-1.313***	-1.520***
	(0.002)	(0.009)
N	2,135,437	1,428,624

**p* < 0.1; ***p* < 0.05; ****p* < 0.01; Robust standard errors in parentheses

Table 3.13 Average adjusted predictions, former politicians in firm

Variables	*Average adjusted predictions*	*Average adjusted predictions*
0bn.*topregulatedind*#0bn.*recession*	0.095***	0.098***
	(0.000)	(0.000)
0bn.*topregulatedind*#1.*recession*	0.085***	0.084***
	(0.001)	(0.001)
1.*topregulatedind*#0bn.*recession*	0.107***	0.123***
	(0.000)	(0.001)
1.*topregulatedind*#1.*recession*	0.106***	0.120***
	(0.001)	(0.001)
N	2,135,437	1,428,624

**p* < 0.1; ***p* < 0.05; ****p* < 0.01

politically connected firms over the period 1999–2014, is used. Based on the author's definition of political connection, the two sides of the revolving door are identified, by focusing on the movement from politics to

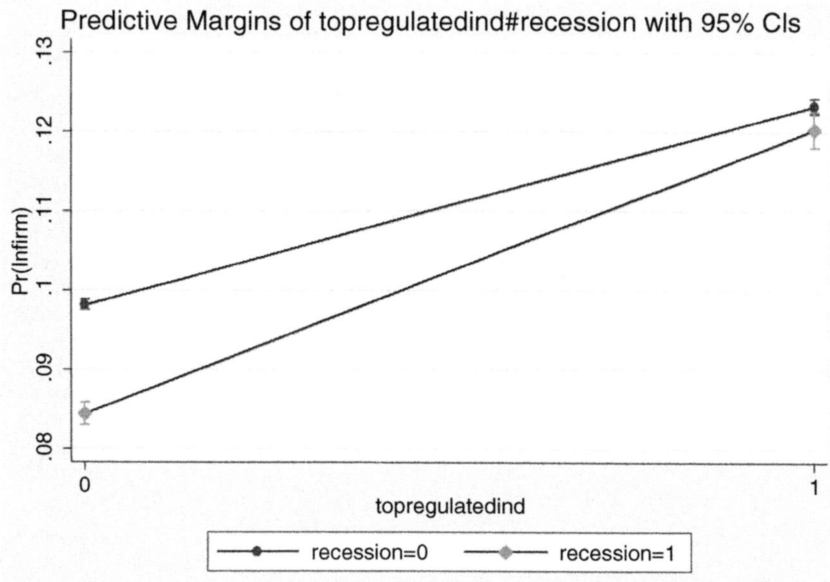

Fig. 3.2 Predictive margins, former politicians in firm

firms and vice versa. Such a definition allows to investigate if firms in the most regulated industries are more likely to be politically connected by considering both trends. Furthermore, recession times are identified according to NBER.

The findings from the cross-sectional probit regressions show that firms belonging to highly regulated industries are more likely to be politically connected, but only by considering former politicians joining firms. By taking into account the phases of economic cycles in the analysis, the probability to be politically connected increases when the industry is heavily regulated and a recession does not occur, by considering both sides of the revolving door. The results seem to suggest that the industry-level regulation matters in establishing political connections, regardless of the occurrence of a recession. Some may ask if the results provide evidence of a causal link between firms belonging to top regulated industries and the probability of being politically connected. Answering this question affirmatively implies the resolution of possible endogeneity problems, as the results may merely be explained by unobserved firms' characteristics which are the primary

Table 3.14 Pooled probit model, former businessmen in politics

Dependent variable: inpolitics	*Coef.*	*Coef.*
0b.*topregulatedind*#1.*recession*	0.070***	0.070***
	(0.006)	(0.006)
1.*topregulatedind*#0b.*recession*	0.181***	0.205***
	(0.004)	(0.004)
1.*topregulatedind*#1.*recession*	0.194***	0.143***
	(0.007)	(0.008)
Leverage2		0.194***
		(0.007)
Roa2		-0.211***
		(0.016)
Size		0.024***
		(0.001)
CIncR2		0.217***
		(0.008)
_cons	-1.891***	-2.207***
	(0.002)	(0.013)
N	2,135,437	1,428,624

$^{*}p < 0.1$; $^{**}p < 0.05$; $^{***}p < 0.01$; Robust standard errors in parentheses

Table 3.15 Average adjusted predictions, former businessmen in politics

Variables	*Average adjusted predictions*	*Average adjusted predictions*
0bn.*topregulatedind*#0bn.*recession*	0.029***	0.035***
	(0.000)	(0.000)
0bn.*topregulatedind*#1.*recession*	0.034***	0.041***
	(0.000)	(0.001)
1.*topregulatedind*#0bn.*recession*	0.044***	0.054***
	(0.000)	(0.000)
1.*topregulatedind*#1.*recession*	0.045***	0.048***
	(0.001)	(0.001)
N	2,135,437	1,428,624

$^{*}p < 0.1$; $^{**}p < 0.05$; $^{***}p < 0.01$

cause of the increased probability. Exploiting a new database, this work provides a first evidence of the existence of a link between industry-level regulation and political connections in the United States. The existence of

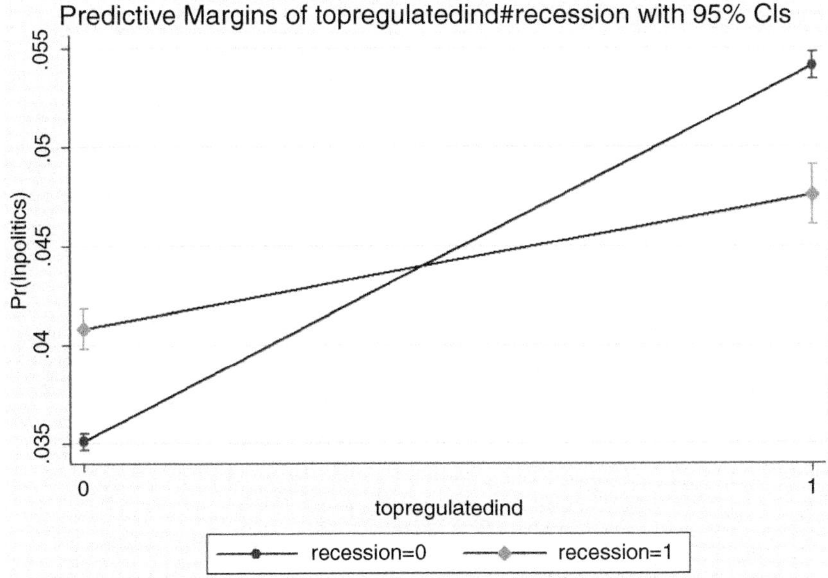

Fig. 3.3 Predictive margins, former businessmen in politics

such a link could be consistent with causality, but the conclusion cannot be considered as definitive at this stage.

Notes

1. From here onward, former directors, corporate executives, and founders entering politics are simply considered as businessmen entering politics.
2. Data are subject to availability. Positions which are frequently accorded cabinet-level rank are considered.
3. As reported on the SEC website (https://www.sec.gov/edgar/searchedgar/cik.htm), CIK is used to identify both corporations and people having filed disclosure with the SEC.
4. Since data are downloaded by using a list of Ticker symbols, those firms are selected, too.
5. With respect to the fiscal year end, financial statement data are lagged by 1 year plus 90 days (the deadline for the publicly traded companies to submit annual reports to the SEC).

CHAPTER 4

Political Connections, Regulation, and Political Party

Abstract In this chapter, only one side of the revolving door (specifically, the one identifying the movement from politics to firms) is taken into account. Moreover, the focus is on the main political parties in the United States (the Republican and the Democratic Parties). Specifically, the point is that a firm should be particularly motivated to either hire or appoint a former politician affiliated with the Republican Party, relying on the belief that Republicans are generally thought of as being pro-business. Therefore, the aim is now to investigate whether listed firms in highly regulated industries are more likely to either hire or appoint a former politician affiliated with the Republican Party. In addition, it is investigated whether highly regulated firms are more likely to either hire or appoint a former politician affiliated with the Republicans when the Republican Party is "strong". The analysis is repeated by considering the Democratic Party. To identify when a Political Party is strong, period of times in which either Republicans have the majority in the Congress and the President is Republican, or Democrats have the majority in the Congress and the President is Democratic, over the period 1999–2014, are selected. The results show that both political affiliation and political environment matter.

Keywords highly regulated firms · political connections · Political Parties

M. Carboni, *The Financial Impact of Political Connections*,
DOI 10.1007/978-3-319-52776-5_4

4.1 Introduction

In the third chapter, it is shown that political connections are more likely to be established if firms operate in highly regulated industries. Starting from that result, this chapter takes into account only one side of the revolving door (from politics to firms). Furthermore, the focus is on the main political parties in the United States (the Republican and Democratic Parties). Specifically, a firm should be particularly interested in either hiring or appointing a former politician affiliated with the Republican Party, relying on the belief that Republicans are generally thought of as being pro-business. Hence, this chapter aims to investigate whether listed firms in highly regulated industries are more likely to either hire or appoint a former politician affiliated with the Republican Party (first research question). Furthermore, it is investigated if firms in highly regulated industries are more likely to either hire or appoint a former politician affiliated with the Republican Party when the latter has the majority in the Congress and it is also the President's affiliated party (second research question). The analysis is repeated for the Democratic Party. The results show that the probability to either hire or appoint a former politician affiliated with the Republican Party increases for firms operating in highly regulated industries. Furthermore, firms are more likely to either hire or appoint a former politician affiliated with Republicans when that political party has the majority in the Congress and the President is Republican, too. Conversely, the probability to either hire or appoint a former politician affiliated with the Democratic Party is higher if the firm does not operate in a top regulated industry, Democrats do not have the majority in the Congress, and the President is not Democratic.

As in the previous chapter, RegData (Al-Ubaydli and McLaughlin 2015) is used in order to identify exhaustively the most regulated industries and therefore investigate whether highly regulated firms are more prone to either hire or appoint a former Republican (Democrat). In addition, it is investigated whether highly regulated firms are more likely to either hire or appoint a former Republican (Democrat) when that party is "strong". Specifically, by exploiting a unique dataset, intervals in which either Republicans have the majority in the Congress and the President is Republican, or Democrats have the majority in the Congress and the President is Democratic, over the period 1999–2014, are identified.

The remainder of the chapter is organized as follows. Section 4.2 describes the sample; Section 4.3 presents the methodology and the variables; Section 4.4 provides the results; and Section 4.5 concludes.

4.2 Sample

To build the sample, the dataset introduced in the third chapter is used. Therefore, as in the previous analysis, politicians in office in the period January 2000–September 2014 related to both the US Legislative (the Senate and the House of Representatives) and Executive Branches (The President, The Vice President, the principal executives of the Executive Office of the President, The Cabinet) are taken into account. Then only politicians who embraced a "business career" as directors and/or corporate executives after leaving politics are selected, and the related listed firms are defined as being "politically connected". The final sample is described in Table 4.1.

4.3 Methodology and variables

To answer the first research question, a pooled probit model is used to investigate whether firms in highly regulated industries are more likely to either hire former politicians affiliated with the Republican Party as corporate executives or appoint them as directors. Afterward, to answer the second research question, an interaction variable is created, by considering the industry-level regulation and the "strength" of Republicans in each time period,

Table 4.1 Sample

No. of firms that have either hired or appointed at least one former Republican over the period 1999–2014	*No. of firms that have either hired or appointed at least one former Democrat over the period 1999–2014*	*No. of firms that have either hired or appointed both former Republicans and Democrats over the period 1999–2014*	*Not possible to define an affiliation with a Political Party*	*Total number of listed firms**
99 (a)	52 (b)	9 (c)	13 (d)	173 (a + b + c + d)**

*Former Republicans and Democrats are former politicians (namely, former member of US Legislative Branch and Executive Branch), selected because in office during the period January 2000–September 2014.

**3 firms are excluded from the sample since the construction of the control variables is not possible for them.

Source: Author's own

with the aim to investigate whether connections with the Republican Party are more likely to be established when firms are subject to high-level regulation, when Republicans have the majority in the Congress and the President is also a Republican. The same analysis is applied to the Democratic Party.

The variables used in the model are defined as follows:

rep is a dummy variable taking value 1 during the days in which a former Republican is working (as director or corporate executive) for a firm (from the date of the announcement, of from the first available date), and 0 otherwise.

dem is a dummy variable taking value 1 during the days in which a former Democrat is working (as director or corporate executive) for a firm (from the date of the announcement, of from the first available date), and 0 otherwise.

rep and *dem* are used as dependent variables in the pooled probit regressions.

control3rep is a dummy variable taking value 1 when Republicans have the majority in both Senate and House, and the President is Republican (by considering the election date), and 0 otherwise.

control3dem is a dummy variable taking value 1 when Democrats have the majority in both Senate and House, and the President is Democratic (by considering the election date), and 0 otherwise.

topregulatedind is a dummy variable taking value 1 if the industry is highly regulated, and 0 otherwise. By using RegData, the 15 most regulated industries for every year, going from 1999 to 2014, are selected. By 3 digit-naics, they are: Chemical Manufacturing (325); Professional, Scientific, and Technical Services (541); Utilities (221); Transportation Equipment Manufacturing (336); Food Manufacturing (311); Support Activities for Transportation (488); Securities, Commodity Contracts, and Other Financial Investments and Related Activities (523); Petroleum and Coal Products Manufacturing (324); Credit Intermediation and Related Activities (522); Air Transportation (481); Animal Production (112); Oil and Gas Extraction (211); Water Transportation (483); Ambulatory Health Care Services (621); Telecommunications (517); and Fishing, Hunting, and Trapping (114). Data on financial statements from financial firms and utilities are different from others, and thereby not properly comparable with those of companies operating in other industries. Consequently, financial firms and utilities are excluded from the regressions when controls for firms' characteristics are added. Furthermore, nonoperating establishments are excluded.

As in the third chapter, firms' characteristics are added in the model, likewise defined as follows:

Leverage2. Following Gorodnichenko and Weber (2016), leverage is computed as the ratio of long-term debt and debt in current liabilities to stockholders' equity, long-term debt, and debt in current liabilities. Leverage is an annual data, and it is lagged in the model. In particular, it is aligned with the data observable by the investors. *Leverage2* is leverage after the winsorization at 1 and 99 percentile levels.

Roa2. Roa is the ratio between pretax income and total assets. It is an annual data, and it is lagged in the model. In particular, it is aligned with the data observable by the investors. *Roa2* is Roa after the winsorization at 1 and 99 percentile levels.

Size. *Size* is the natural log of total assets. It is an annual data, and it is lagged in the model. In particular, it is aligned with the data observable by the investors.

CIncR2. *CIncR* is the ratio between cost of goods sold and sales/turnover (net). It is an annual data, and it is lagged in the model. In particular, it is aligned with the data observable by the investors. *CIncR2* is *CIncR* after the winsorization at 1 and 99 percentile levels.

Table 4.2 summarizes the variables along with a description of each variable used in the analysis.

4.4 Results

Table 4.3 presents the results of the pooled probit regressions. First, the probability of a firm from a highly regulated industry to either hire former politicians affiliated with the Republican Party or appoint them as directors is investigated. The results are reported in the first column. Then the regression is rerun by controlling for firms' characteristics (second column). In both cases, the coefficient of *topregulatedind* is positive and significant at 1% level, suggesting that the likelihood of firms to either hire former politicians affiliated with the Republican Party or appoint them as directors is associated with its belonging to a top regulated industry. Furthermore, in order to investigate if the "strength" of Republicans matters, an interaction variable between *topregulatedind* and *control3rep* is created and the regression is rerun.

Table 4.2 List and definition of variables

Variable	*Variable definition*
rep	A dummy variable = 1 during the days in which a former Republican is working (as director or corporate executive) for a firm (from the date of the announcement, of from the first available date), and 0 otherwise.
dem	A dummy variable = 1 during the days in which a former Democrat is working (as director or corporate executive) for a firm (from the date of the announcement, of from the first available date), and 0 otherwise.
control3rep	A dummy variable = 1 when Republicans have the majority in Senate and House of Representatives, and the President is Republican (by considering the election date), and 0 otherwise.
control3dem	A dummy variable = 1 when Democrats have the majority in Senate and House of Representatives, and the President is Democratic (by considering the election date), and 0 otherwise.
topregulatedind	A dummy variable = 1 if the industry is heavily regulated, and 0 otherwise. By using RegData, the 15 most regulated industries for each year, going from 1999 to 2014, have been selected. By 3 digit-naics, the most regulated industries are: Chemical Manufacturing (325), Professional, Scientific, and Technical Services (541); Utilities (221); Transportation Equipment Manufacturing (336); Food Manufacturing (311); Support Activities for Transportation (488); Securities, Commodity Contracts, and Other Financial Investments and Related Activities (523); Petroleum and Coal Products Manufacturing (324); Credit Intermediation and Related Activities (522); Air Transportation (481); Animal Production (112); Oil and Gas Extraction (211); Water Transportation (483), Ambulatory Health Care Services (621); Telecommunications (517); Fishing, Hunting, and Trapping (114).
Leverage2	Leverage is the ratio of long-term debt and debt in current liabilities to stockholders' equity, long-term debt, and debt in current liabilities. Leverage is an annual data, and it is lagged in the model. In particular, it is aligned with the data observable by the investors. *Leverage2* is leverage after the winsorization at 1 and 99 percentile levels.

Table 4.2 (continued)

Variable	*Variable definition*
Roa2	Roa is the ratio between pretax income and total assets. It is an annual data, and it is lagged in the model. In particular, it is aligned with the data observable by the investors. *Roa2* is Roa after the winsorization at 1 and 99 percentile levels.
Size	*Size* is the natural log of total assets. It is an annual data, and it is lagged in the model. In particular, it is aligned with the data observable by the investors.
CIncR2	CIncR is the ratio between cost of goods sold and sales/turnover (net). It is an annual data, and it is lagged in the model. In particular, it is aligned with the data observable by the investors. *CIncR2* is CIncR after the winsorization at 1 and 99 percentile levels.

Source: Author's own

Table 4.3 Pooled probit model, former republicans in firm

Dependent variable: rep	*Coef.*	*Coef.*	*Coef.*	*Coef.*
1.*topregulatedind*	0.269***	0.465***		
	(0.006)	(0.008)		
Leverage2		-0.612***		-0.595***
		(0.013)		(0.013)
Roa2		-0.062***		-0.055***
		(0.018)		(0.018)
Size		-0.114***		-0.118***
		(0.002)		(0.002)
CIncR2		-0.013***		-0.026***
		(0.003)		(0.003)
0b.*topregulatedind*#1.*control3rep*			-0.189***	-0.256***
			(0.010)	(0.011)
1.*topregulatedind*#0b.*control3rep*			0.195***	0.376***
			(0.007)	(0.008)
1.*topregulatedind*#1.*control3rep*			0.463***	0.718***
			(0.014)	(0.018)
_cons	0.264***	1.540***	0.304***	1.631***
	(0.004)	(0.018)	(0.004)	(0.019)
N	188,309	140,628	188,309	140,628

**p* < 0.1; ***p* < 0.05; ****p* < 0.01; Robust standard errors in parentheses

The results are reported in the third column. The fourth column includes firms' characteristics.

Table 4.4 shows the average adjusted predictions. The probability to either hire former politicians affiliated with the Republican Party or appoint them as directors is higher if a firm operates in a top regulated industry compared to the case in which it does not (first column). The effect is basically unchanged after controlling for firms' characteristics (second column). Table 4.5 shows the average marginal effects with

Table 4.4 Former republicans in firm, average adjusted predictions

Variables	*Average adjusted predictions*	*Average adjusted predictions*	*Average adjusted predictions*	*Average adjusted predictions*
0bn.*topregulatedind*	0.604***	0.620***		
	(0.002)	(0.002)		
1.*topregulatedind*	0.703***	0.773***		
	(0.002)	(0.002)		
0bn.*topregulatedind*#0bn.*control3rep*			0.619***	0.639***
			(0.002)	(0.002)
0bn.*topregulatedind*#1.*control3rep*			0.546***	0.545***
			(0.003)	(0.004)
1.*topregulatedind*#0bn.*control3rep*			0.691***	0.763***
			(0.002)	(0.002)
1.*topregulatedind*#1.*control3rep*			0.778***	0.851***
			(0.004)	(0.004)
N	188,309	140,628	188,309	140,628

*$p < 0.1$; **$p < 0.05$; ***$p < 0.01$

Table 4.5 Former republicans in firm, average marginal effects

Variables	*Average marginal effects*
1.*topregulatedind*	0.153***
	(0.002)
N	140,628

*$p < 0.1$; **$p < 0.05$; ***$p < 0.01$

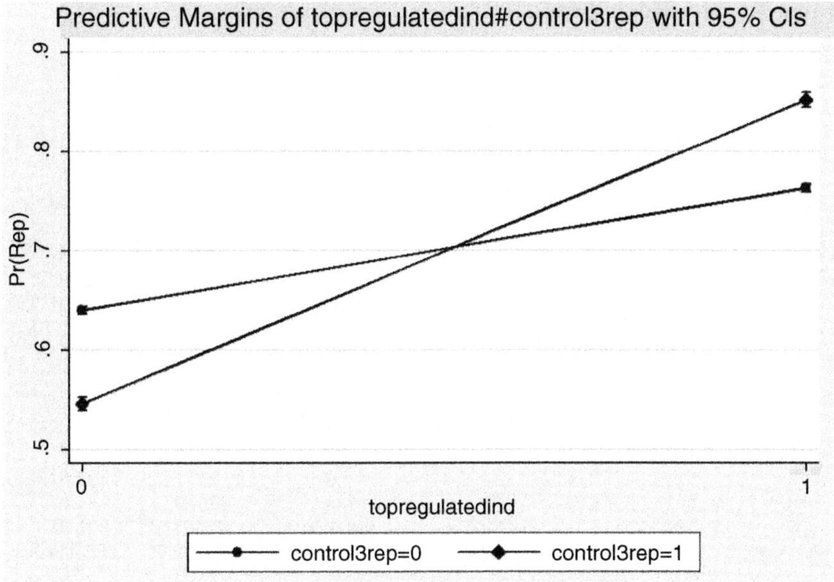

Fig. 4.1 Predictive margins, former republicans in firm

respect to the last case. Furthermore, the probability to either hire former politicians affiliated with the Republican Party or appoint them as directors is higher if a firm operates in a top regulated industry, if Republicans have the majority in the Congress, and the President is also Republican (Table 4.4, third column). The effect is basically unchanged after controlling for firms' characteristics (fourth column). Figure 4.1 displays the predictive margins with respect to the last case.

The analysis is repeated for the Democratic Party (Table 4.6). The coefficient of *topregulatedind* is negative and significant at 1% level (first column), also after controlling for firms' characteristics (second column). The results suggest that the probability of a firm to either hire former politicians affiliated with the Democratic Party or appoint them as directors is negatively associated with its belonging to a top regulated industry. Furthermore, in order to investigate if the "strength" of the party matters, an interaction variable between *topregulatedind* and *control3dem* is created and the regression is rerun. The results are reported in the third column. The fourth column includes firms' characteristics.

Table 4.6 Pooled probit model, former democrats in firm

Dependent variable: Dem	*Coef.*	*Coef.*	*Coef.*	*Coef.*
1.*topregulatedind*	-0.217***	-0.402***		
	(0.006)	(0.008)		
Leverage2		0.615***		0.612***
		(0.013)		(0.013)
Roa2		0.038**		0.033*
		(0.018)		(0.018)
Size		0.128***		0.128***
		(0.002)		(0.002)
CIncR2		0.018***		0.017***
		(0.003)		(0.003)
0b.*topregulatedind*#1.*control3dem*			-0.062***	-0.048***
			(0.011)	(0.012)
1.*topregulatedind*#0b.*control3dem*			-0.227***	-0.416***
			(0.007)	(0.008)
1.*topregulatedind*#1.*control3dem*			-0.227***	-0.390***
			(0.011)	(0.013)
_cons	-0.199***	-1.645***	-0.189***	-1.636***
	(0.004)	(0.018)	(0.004)	(0.018)
N	188,309	140,628	188,309	140,628

$^{*}p < 0.1$; $^{**}p < 0.05$; $^{***}p < 0.01$; Robust standard errors in parentheses

Table 4.7 shows the average adjusted predictions. The probability to either hire former politicians affiliated with the Democratic Party or appoint them as directors is lower if the industry belongs to a top regulated industry with respect to the case in which it does not (first column), also after controlling for firms' characteristics (second column). Table 4.8 shows the average marginal effects with respect to the last case. Furthermore, the probability to either hire former politicians affiliated with the Democratic Party or appoint them as directors is higher if the firm does not belong to a top regulated industry, the Democrats do not have the majority in the Congress, and the President is not Democratic (Table 4.7, third column), also after controlling for firms' characteristics (fourth column). Figure 4.2 shows the predictive margins with respect to the last case.

4.5 Conclusions

In the fourth chapter, first it is asked whether firms belonging to the top regulated industries are more likely to either hire former politicians affiliated with the Republican Party or to appoint them as directors.

Table 4.7 Former democrats in firm, average adjusted predictions

Variables	*Average adjusted predictions*	*Average adjusted predictions*	*Average adjusted predictions*	*Average adjusted predictions*
0bn.*topregulatedind*	0.421***	0.389***		
	(0.002)	(0.002)		
1.*topregulatedind*	0.339***	0.254***		
	(0.002)	(0.002)		
0bn.*topregulatedind*#0bn.*control3dem*			0.425***	0.392***
			(0.002)	(0.002)
0bn.*topregulatedind*#1.*control3dem*			0.401***	0.374***
			(0.004)	(0.004)
1.*topregulatedind*#0bn.*control3dem*			0.338***	0.252***
			(0.002)	(0.002)
1.*topregulatedind*#1.*control3dem*			0.339***	0.260***
			(0.004)	(0.004)
N	188,309	140,628	188,309	140,628

*$p < 0.1$; **$p < 0.05$; ***$p < 0.01$

Table 4.8 Former democrats in firm, average marginal effects

Variables	*Average marginal effects*
1.*topregulatedind*	−0.135***
	(0.002)
N	140,628

*$p < 0.1$; **$p < 0.05$; ***$p < 0.01$

Next, it is investigated if the probability to either hire former politicians affiliated with the Republicans or appoint them as directors increases depending not only on the industry-level regulation, but also on the "strength" of that political party. In particular, the reference is to the case in which Republicans have the majority in the Congress and the President is also Republican. The analysis is repeated for the Democratic Party.

To address each question, a unique database is used, allowing to identify firms either hiring or appointing former politicians in office over the period 2000–2014.

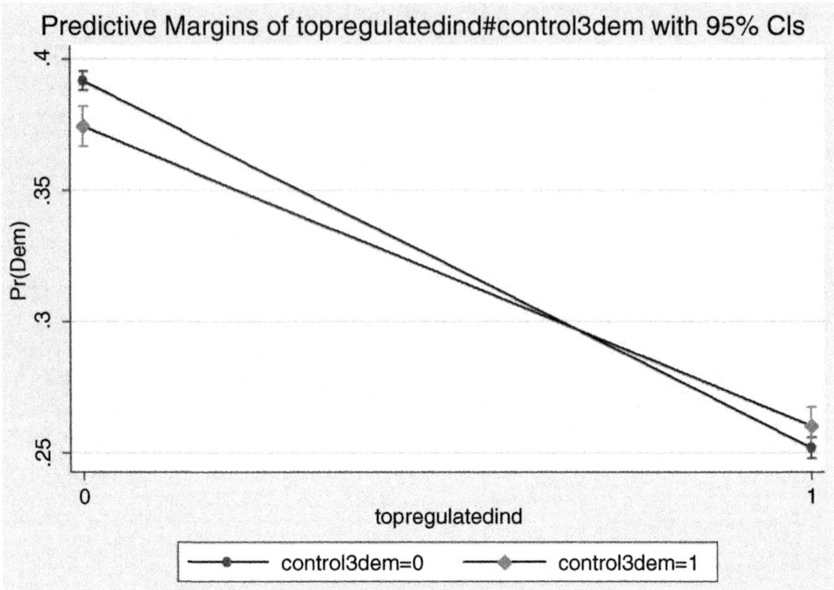

Fig. 4.2 Predictive margins, former democrats in firm

Findings from this research suggest that the probability to either hire or appoint former politicians affiliated with the Republican Party, commonly thought of as being pro-business, is higher if the industry is highly regulated. In addition, the probability to either hire former politicians affiliated with the Republican Party or appoint them as directors is higher if the industry is highly regulated, if Republicans have the majority in the Congress, and the President is also Republican. Opposite results are obtained for the Democratic Party, as the probability to either hire former politicians affiliated with this Party or appoint them as directors is higher if a firm does not belong to a top regulated industry. In addition, the probability to either hire former politicians affiliated with the Democratic Party or appoint them as directors is higher if a firm does not belong to a top regulated industry, Democrats do not have the majority in the Congress, and the President is not Democratic. Overall, the findings show that both political affiliation and political environment matter.

CHAPTER 5

Political Connections and Firm Value

Abstract In this chapter, the market reaction to the announcement of a new political connection is investigated. Because of the author's definition of political connection, the sample is first considered entirely and then divided in order to analyze the investors' reaction following the announcement of former politicians joining firms and former businessmen entering politics. Afterward, two more subsamples are considered: first, the top contractors in the United States and second, companies operating in highly regulated industries. To analyze if the stock returns of the firms in the sample and subsamples display abnormal returns (ARs) around the announcement day of a new political connection, the event study approach is employed. The results are consistent with the view that the industry-level regulation matters.

Keywords event study · firm value · political connections

5.1 Introduction

This chapter aims to investigate the market reaction at the announcement of a new political connection. The sample is first entirely considered, and then, based on the definition of political connection provided in the third chapter, it is divided in order to investigate the investors' reaction at the announcement of former politicians joining firms and former businessmen entering politics (that is, by considering both sides of the revolving door separately). In addition, two subsamples are considered. The first one consists of the top

M. Carboni, *The Financial Impact of Political Connections*,
DOI 10.1007/978-3-319-52776-5_5

contractors in the United States, while the second one is composed of companies operating in highly regulated industries. The findings show that a positive and significant reaction exists, but only if former politicians join firms and if firms are either top contractors or highly regulated. The results are consistent with the view that the industry-level regulation matters.

The remainder of the chapter is organized as follows. Section 5.2 describes the sample; Section 5.3 presents the methodology; Section 5.4 provides the results; and Section 5.5 concludes.

5.2 Sample

The hand-collected dataset introduced in the third chapter is exploited. For this analysis, the sample consists of 159 firms, with a total number of 213 announcements of former politicians joining firms (136 announcements) and former businessmen entering politics (77 announcements). Observations are excluded if: (i) they are confounded by other relevant firm-level news (such as mergers or spinoffs occurring on the announcement day); (ii) the stock market is closed; (iii) the day of the announcement in newspapers is chronologically posterior with respect to the date on filings provided by the EDGAR database, if available (such an exclusion is motivated by the presence of a clear anticipatory effect). As previously explained, the dates of announcement of corporate and political appointments are collected by performing an extensive keyword search on LexisNexis. Moreover, politicians are related to both US Legislative (the Senate and the House of Representatives) and Executive Branches (the President, the Vice President, the principal executives of the Executive Office of the President, the Cabinet), and are in office over the period January 2000–September 2014. In the sample, 64 out of 213 announcements are related to firms included in the 2014 top 100 contractors report.[1] Specifically, 38 out of 64 announcements are related to former politicians joining firms, and 26 out of 64 announcements are related to former businessmen entering politics. Furthermore, by using RegData (Al-Ubaydli and McLaughlin 2015), the most regulated industries by selecting the top 15 regulated industries from 1999–2014 are identified. By considering the full sample, 112 out of 213 announcements are related to firms in highly regulated industries. Specifically, 69 announcements out of 112 are related to former politicians joining firms, and the difference is related to former businessmen entering politics (43 announcements). The sample is described in Tables from 5.1 to 5.3.

Table 5.1 Sample

Total no. of announcements, both sides of the revolving door	*Former politicians in firm*	*Former businessmen in politics*
213 (a + b)	136 (a)	77 (b)

Source: Author's own

Table 5.2 Subsample (1) firms among the top 100 contractors

Total no. of announcements, both sides of the revolving door	*Former politicians in firm*	*Former businessmen in politics*
64 (c + d)	38 (c)	26 (d)

Source: Author's own

Table 5.3 Subsample (2) firms in top regulated industries

Total no. of announcements, both sides of the revolving door	*Former politicians in firm*	*Former businessmen in politics*
112 (e + f)	69 (e)	43(f)

Source: Author's own

5.3 Methodology

An event study is run in order to analyze if the stock returns of the firms in the sample display ARs around the announcement day of a new political connection. Daily ARs can be computed through the use of several benchmarks.[2] Following Amici et al. (2013), "normal" returns are estimated by adopting the market model. It predicts returns in "normal" conditions:

$$R_{it} = \alpha_{\mathrm{i}} + \beta_i R_{\mathrm{M}t} + \varepsilon_{\mathrm{it}} \quad \text{with } E(\varepsilon_{it}) = 0 \text{ and } \mathrm{var}(\varepsilon_{\mathrm{it}}) = \sigma^2_{\varepsilon_{\mathrm{i}}} \tag{1}$$

where: R_{it} is the daily log return for every ith firm at time t ("normal" return) and $\mathrm{R}_{\mathrm{M}t}$ is the return of the market index at time t (in this study, S&P 500 Index is used). Market model parameters (α_i and β_i)

are obtained with an ordinary least squares (OLS) regression over a 252-day estimation period, ending 20 days before the announcement, that is, the *estimation window*. Such a window can be considered as a normal period by making the hypothesis that returns more than 20 days before the announcement are not affected by the event. Time series with an insufficient length of the estimation period have been excluded. Moreover, illiquid stocks have been dropped (at least one stock price variation must occur every week).

Once the estimated values of α_i and β_i are obtained, predicted returns in the *event window* (namely, in the interval of time containing the day of the event + n days prior to and/or after the event) can be found by plugging in the market return. Therefore, the difference between actual and predicted returns (namely, the predicted returns by the model) at every point in the considered event window provides daily ARs:

$$AR_{it} = R_{it} - \hat{\alpha}_i - \hat{\beta}_i R_{Mt} \tag{2}$$

By assuming that the announcement date is $t = 0$, the focus is on the AR in the day of the event and on the following short event window: (−1; +1). In addition, both the cases that the announcement may be forecast by investors and the stock reaction may be longer (delayed reaction) are included in the analysis. Therefore, the following event windows are also considered: (−1, +3), (−3, +3), (−5, +5), (−3, +5), (−3, +1), (−1, +5) plus two more event windows: (0; +1) and (−1; 0).

ARs are summed over a time period around the event in order to obtain the CARs. Therefore, for each event window, CARs are computed in the following way:

$$CAR_i(W) = \sum_{t=t_1}^{t_2} AR_{it} \tag{3}$$

where t_1 and t_2 are the start and the end dates of each window W.

ARs can be also aggregated on a cross-sectional basis for a portfolio of N firms; therefore, for each event window, the cumulative average abnormal return (CAAR) is computed as follows:

$$CAAR(W) = \frac{1}{N}\sum_{i=1}^{N} CAR_i(W) \tag{4}$$

Once CAARs are obtained, the hypothesis of a market reaction significantly different from zero is tested (the null hypothesis is a market reaction equal to zero).

Several studies have highlighted an increase in variance in ARs in the days close to the event, as a consequence of the announcement itself (Cummins and Weiss 2004). As properly noted in Amici et al. (2013), such a phenomenon needs to be taken into account in hypothesis testing. Consequently, the methodology suggested by Mikkelson and Partch (1988) and then used in other studies (for example, Harrington and Shrider 2007; Mentz and Schiereck 2008) is adopted, suggesting to employ the Boehmer et al. (1991) test statistic. First, a standardization factor is computed (Amici et al. 2013, p. 1389):

$$SR_i = \frac{CAR_i(t_1, t_2)}{\hat{\sigma}_{\varepsilon_i}\sqrt{T_S + \frac{T_S^2}{T} + \frac{\sum_{t=t_1}^{t_2}(R_{Mt} - T_S(\bar{R}_M))^2}{\sum_{t=1}^{T}(R_{Mt} - \bar{R}_M)^2}}}$$

where:
$\hat{\sigma}_{\varepsilon_i}$ is the standard deviation of ARs estimated through the market model;
T_S is the number of days in the event window;
T is the number of days in the considered estimation period;
R_{Mt} is the market portfolio return at time t; and
$\bar{R}_M$ is the average market portfolio return in the considered estimation period.

Second, the *Z*-statistic (having a t-distribution with T – 2 degrees of freedom and converging to a unit normal) is defined as follows (Amici et al. 2013, p. 1389):

$$Z = \frac{\frac{1}{N}\sum_{i=1}^{N} SR_i}{\sqrt{\frac{1}{N(N-1)}\sum_{i=1}^{N}\left(SR_i - \sum_{i=1}^{N}\frac{SR_i}{N}\right)^2}}$$

Kolari and Pynnönen (2010) suggest a test statistic aiming to account for the presence of cross-sectional correlation among ARs. The adjusted test statistic is then obtained through the application of the following correction factor to Z (Amici et al. 2013, p. 1390):

$$\sqrt{\frac{1-\bar{r}}{1+(N-1)\bar{r}}}$$

where $\bar{r}$ is the mean of the cross correlations of the estimation period residuals and N is the number of companies in the sample.

5.4 Results

This section presents the findings. In each table, estimated CAARs for different event windows, results of the test of significance, minimum and maximum CARs, and percentages of positive CARs are reported. The statistical significance of CAARs is tested by employing the Boehmer et al. (1991) methodology with the inclusion of adjustment proposed by Kolari and Pynnönen (2010), in order to account respectively for the increase in variance in ARs in the days close to the event, caused by the event itself, and the presence of cross-sectional correlation among ARs.

Table 5.4 shows the results of the event study following the announcements of a new political connection, by considering both sides of the revolving door. The sample is slightly reduced with respect to the initial number (213 observations), since both the insufficiently long time series and the illiquid stocks are dropped. Finally, 206 dates are obtained, consisting of 129 announcements of former politicians joining firms (Table 5.5) and 77 announcements of former businessmen entering politics (Table 5.6). Across all the event windows, estimated CAARs are never statistically significant at the 10% level or less, also after having distinguished between the two sides of the revolving door. The hypothesis test fails to reject the null hypothesis, suggesting that the announcements do not create firm value. One possible explanation for the results lays in the high predictability of political outcomes in the United States. This characteristic, however, explains only the findings related to one side of the revolving door, namely the one

Table 5.4 Announcement of a new political connection full sample both sides of the revolving door

N = 206	*CAARs*	*Z-stat.*	*P-value*	*Min(%)*	*Max(%)*	*Pos(%)*
(−1,3)	0.20%	0.2644	0.791477	-23.20%	22.92%	49.51%
(−1,1)	0.00%	-0.3717	0.710121	-15.76%	30.70%	48.06%
(0,1)	0.04%	-0.0848	0.932407	-16.63%	26.80%	52.43%
(0)	-0.10%	-0.7936	0.427403	-9.20%	10.59%	43.69%
(−1,0)	-0.13%	-0.9653	0.334412	-11.09%	8.90%	45.63%
(−3,3)	0.19%	0.2374	0.812352	-26.90%	19.46%	50.49%
(−5,5)	0.28%	0.1859	0.852523	-32.75%	24.52%	47.09%
(−3,5)	0.09%	0.1998	0.841606	-30.33%	22.92%	50.00%
(−3,1)	-0.01%	-0.2683	0.788479	-19.46%	27.24%	50.97%
(−1,5)	0.10%	0.2051	0.837526	-33.90%	30.70%	51.46%

Source: Author's own

Table 5.5 Announcement of a new political connection full sample former politicians join firms

N = 129	*CAARs*	*Z-stat.*	*P-value*	*Min(%)*	*Max(%)*	*Pos(%)*
(−1,3)	0.06%	0.4758	0.634187	-13.69%	21.24%	50.39%
(−1,1)	-0.02%	0.1110	0.911640	-12.37%	13.98%	52.71%
(0,1)	0.09%	0.4107	0.681311	-10.82%	15.67%	55.81%
(0)	-0.03%	-0.4773	0.633181	-6.83%	10.59%	43.41%
(−1,0)	-0.14%	-0.5733	0.566424	-11.09%	8.90%	45.74%
(−3,3)	-0.13%	-0.0024	0.998120	-18.46%	13.45%	50.39%
(−5,5)	0.22%	0.0811	0.935385	-21.82%	24.52%	49.61%
(−3,5)	-0.05%	-0.1440	0.885492	-21.05%	22.92%	48.06%
(−3,1)	-0.20%	-0.3792	0.704532	-16.92%	15.29%	51.16%
(−1,5)	0.14%	0.2217	0.824576	-18.70%	30.70%	50.39%

Source: Author's own

describing the movement from business to politics (that is, related to former businessmen entering politics).

Table 5.7 shows the results of the first subsample (regarding the announcements of a new political connection for firms that are among the top 100 contractors). CAARs are positive in all event windows, but they are not statistically significant. When a distinction is made between the two sides of the revolving door, the analysis indicates the existence of more favorable CAARs (positive and statistically

Table 5.6 Announcement of a new political connection full sample former businessmen in politics

N = 77	*CAARs*	*Z-stat.*	*P-value*	*Min(%)*	*Max(%)*	*Pos(%)*
(−1,3)	0.45%	−0.1334	0.893850	−23.20%	22.92%	48.05%
(−1,1)	0.03%	−0.6271	0.530585	−15.76%	30.70%	40.26%
(0,1)	−0.05%	−0.4923	0.622538	−16.63%	26.80%	46.75%
(0)	−0.21%	−0.6328	0.526835	−9.20%	8.32%	44.16%
(−1,0)	−0.12%	−0.8070	0.419689	−8.52%	7.95%	45.45%
(−3,3)	0.71%	0.3842	0.700801	−26.90%	19.46%	50.65%
(−5,5)	0.38%	0.1976	0.843385	−32.75%	23.10%	42.86%
(−3,5)	0.31%	0.5292	0.596697	−30.33%	20.24%	53.25%
(−3,1)	0.29%	0.0404	0.967776	−19.46%	27.24%	50.65%
(−1,5)	0.05%	0.0552	0.955985	−33.90%	23.70%	53.25%

Table 5.7 Announcement of a new political connection subsample (1) firms are among the top 100 contractors both sides of the revolving door

N = 62	*CAARs*	*Z-stat.*	*P-value*	*Min(%)*	*Max(%)*	*Pos(%)*
(−1,3)	0.15%	0.4887	0.625022	−9.76%	8.00%	46.77%
(−1,1)	0.34%	0.8590	0.390318	−7.50%	7.62%	53.23%
(0,1)	0.25%	0.8061	0.420167	−8.07%	7.49%	61.29%
(0)	0.03%	0.2916	0.770621	−9.20%	8.32%	48.39%
(−1,0)	0.12%	0.4105	0.681465	−8.52%	7.27%	53.23%
(−3,3)	0.43%	1.1501	0.250094	−12.85%	13.16%	54.84%
(−5,5)	0.48%	0.5149	0.606650	−16.25%	19.34%	43.55%
(−3,5)	0.44%	1.0777	0.281147	−19.59%	16.94%	53.23%
(−3,1)	0.62%	1.5922	0.111349	−13.51%	15.29%	58.06%
(−1,5)	0.16%	0.4601	0.645472	−13.48%	8.45%	58.06%

Source: Author's own

significant at the 10% level in both the 5-day and the 7-day event windows) if former politicians join firms (Table 5.8). Table 5.9 shows the results (never significant at the 10% confidence level or less) related to the announcement dates of former businessmen entering politics.

Table 5.10 shows the results of the second subsample (related to announcements of a new political connection for firms in top regulated industries, according to RegData). By focusing on the whole sample (107 observations), estimated CAARs are positive in all event

Table 5.8 Announcement of a new political connection subsample (1) Firms are among the top 100 contractors former politicians in firm

N = 36	*CAARs*	*Z-stat.*	*P-value*	*Min(%)*	*Max(%)*	*Pos(%)*
(-1,3)	**0.50%**	**1.6521**	**0.098511**	**-9.76%**	**7.92%**	**55.56%**
(-1,1)	0.37%	1.0637	0.287469	-7.50%	6.63%	61.11%
(0,1)	0.32%	1.2847	0.198901	-5.03%	5.06%	63.89%
(0)	-0.05%	0.2767	0.781975	-4.29%	4.07%	50.00%
(-1,0)	0.00%	0.3117	0.755269	-4.79%	7.27%	55.56%
(-3,3)	**0.77%**	**1.6466**	**0.099640**	**-12.85%**	**13.16%**	**61.11%**
(-5,5)	0.53%	0.4674	0.640200	-16.25%	19.34%	47.22%
(-3,5)	0.61%	1.0553	0.291282	-17.16%	16.94%	55.56%
(-3,1)	0.65%	1.2058	0.227910	-9.91%	15.29%	55.56%
(-1,5)	0.33%	0.9069	0.364446	-8.80%	7.94%	61.11%

Bold value means that the results are significant.
Source: Author's own

Table 5.9 Announcement of a new political connection subsample (1) firms are among the top 100 contractors former businessmen in politics

N = 26	*CAARs*	*Z-stat.*	*P-value*	*Min(%)*	*Max(%)*	*Pos(%)*
(-1,3)	-0.34%	-0.9471	0.343603	-6.94%	8.00%	34.62%
(-1,1)	0.30%	0.0501	0.960027	-7.40%	7.62%	42.31%
(0,1)	0.16%	-0.0423	0.966223	-8.07%	7.49%	57.69%
(0)	0.15%	0.1221	0.902809	-9.20%	8.32%	46.15%
(-1,0)	0.28%	0.2348	0.814326	-8.52%	5.60%	50.00%
(-3,3)	-0.05%	-0.2348	0.814357	-11.33%	11.44%	46.15%
(-5,5)	0.39%	0.1938	0.846334	-5.22%	12.35%	38.46%
(-3,5)	0.21%	0.3242	0.745797	-19.59%	11.90%	50.00%
(-3,1)	0.59%	0.9134	0.361055	-13.51%	11.07%	61.54%
(-1,5)	-0.08%	-0.2454	0.806142	-13.48%	8.45%	53.85%

Source: Author's own

windows, with the exception of the 7-day event window (−1; +5) and the AR in the day of the announcement (0). However, they are not statistically significant. After dividing the sample, CAARs become positive and statistically significant at the 10% level in the event windows (−1; +1) and (−1; +5), and at 5% level in the event windows (−1; +3) and (−3; +3) when former politicians join firms (Table 5.11). On the other hand, estimated CAARs are not significant when former businessmen enter politics (Table 5.12).

Table 5.10 Announcement of a new political connection subsample (2) firms in top regulated industries both sides of the revolving door

N = 107	*CAARs*	*Z-stat.*	*P-value*	*Min(%)*	*Max(%)*	*Pos(%)*
(-1,3)	0.12%	0.8947	0.370965	-23.20%	21.24%	52.34%
(-1,1)	0.05%	0.6999	0.483993	-15.76%	13.98%	49.53%
(0,1)	0.00%	0.0700	0.944209	-16.63%	15.67%	53.27%
(0)	-0.04%	-0.4966	0.619485	-9.20%	10.59%	45.79%
(-1,0)	0.01%	0.3015	0.763008	-8.52%	8.90%	50.47%
(-3,3)	0.28%	1.0971	0.272603	-26.90%	13.45%	53.27%
(-5,5)	0.29%	0.5661	0.571336	-32.75%	24.52%	46.73%
(-3,5)	0.02%	0.6617	0.508134	-30.33%	22.92%	48.60%
(-3,1)	0.20%	0.9074	0.364177	-19.46%	15.29%	56.07%
(-1,5)	-0.13%	0.4260	0.670133	-33.90%	30.70%	53.27%

Source: Author's own

Table 5.11 Announcement of a new political connection subsample (2) firms in top regulated industries former politicians in firm

N = 64	*CAARs*	*Z-stat.*	*P-value*	*Min(%)*	*Max(%)*	*Pos(%)*
(-1,3)	**0.91%**	**2.5044**	**0.012266**	**-11.04%**	**21.24%**	**60.94%**
(-1,1)	**0.52%**	**1.9018**	**0.057200**	**-11.53%**	**13.98%**	**57.81%**
(0,1)	0.22%	0.7266	0.467481	-7.05%	15.67%	54.69%
(0)	0.01%	-0.3260	0.744459	-4.29%	10.59%	43.75%
(-1,0)	0.31%	1.1128	0.265802	-6.62%	8.90%	56.25%
(-3,3)	**0.89%**	**2.0394**	**0.041411**	**-13.80%**	**13.45%**	**57.81%**
(-5,5)	1.37%	1.4642	0.143145	-19.91%	24.52%	54.69%
(-3,5)	0.86%	1.3897	0.164612	-19.85%	22.92%	50.00%
(-3,1)	0.50%	1.3353	0.181792	-16.21%	15.29%	57.81%
(-1,5)	**0.88%**	**1.6497**	**0.099000**	**-15.17%**	**30.70%**	**56.25%**

Bold value means that the results are significant.
Source: Author's own

5.5 Conclusions

In this chapter, the market reaction at the announcement of a new political connection is analyzed. Specifically, an event study is performed to investigate if stock prices around the event display ARs. The event study approach follows a three-step procedure: (i) compute the daily ARs in the days around the announcement of the event (in

Table 5.12 Announcement of a new political connection subsample (2) firms in top regulated industries former businessmen in politics

N = 43	*CAARs*	*Z-stat.*	*P-value*	*Min(%)*	*Max(%)*	*Pos(%)*
(−1,3)	−1.05%	−1.2091	0.226621	−23.20%	8.00%	39.53%
(−1,1)	−0.65%	−0.9938	0.320317	−15.76%	7.62%	37.21%
(0,1)	−0.32%	−0.5597	0.575705	16.63%	7.49%	51.16%
(0)	−0.12%	−0.3546	0.722902	−9.20%	8.32%	48.84%
(−1,0)	−0.45%	−0.8462	0.397460	−8.52%	5.60%	41.86%
(−3,3)	−0.64%	−0.5988	0.549317	−26.90%	11.44%	46.51%
(−5,5)	−1.31%	−0.9151	0.360135	−32.75%	12.35%	34.88%
(−3,5)	−1.23%	−0.5638	0.572893	−30.33%	11.90%	46.51%
(−3,1)	−0.24%	−0.1565	0.875646	−19.46%	11.07%	53.49%
(−1,5)	−1.64%	−1.0541	0.291821	−33.90%	8.45%	48.84%

Source: Author's own

this study, they are computed by using the market model with a 252-day estimation period); (ii) compute the CARs by aggregating the ARs; and (iii) compute the CAARs, by taking the mean of the CARs. After that, it is possible to test the hypothesis of a market reaction significantly different from zero.

The market reaction is first investigated by considering the full sample, and then by focusing on the two sides of the revolving door separately (that is, announcements of former politicians joining firms and former businessmen entering politics). In all the cases, estimated CAARs are never statistically significant at the 10% level or less, indicating that the announcement of a new political connection does not generate value creation. By considering the first subsample (firms among the top 100 contractors), the results show evidence of a positive and significant reaction for two event windows, but only when former politicians join firms. Furthermore, a second subsample of firms in the most regulated industries is considered. CAARs are never statistically significant when the two sides of the revolving door are taken into account together. Conversely, following announcements of former politicians joining firms, CAARs are positive across all the event windows and show statistical significance in four cases. The absence of a significant response to the announcement of former businessmen entering politics could be plausibly due to the high predictability of political outcomes in the United States.

The main finding of this chapter is that investors detect a new political connection as valuable if firms operate in highly regulated industries, but only when former politicians join firms. The results are consistent with the view that industry-level regulation matters.

Notes

1. "Top 100 Contractors Report", Federal Procurement Data System – Next Generation, accessed: May 31, 2016, https://www.fpds.gov/fpdsng_cms/index.php/en/.
2. See: "Equity Strategy Research - Value Relevance of Analysts' Earnings Forecasts." Accessed January 23, 2017. https://www.princeton.edu/~markus/teaching/Eco467/04Lecture/04Event%20Study%20Description.pdf.

CHAPTER 6

Conclusions

Abstract After giving a definition of connection, based on the movement between politics and business (revolving door), and by exploiting a unique dataset for the period 1999–2014, this book focuses on political connections in the United States. In particular, after a review of the main literature (second chapter), it is asked whether firms belonging to highly regulated industries are more likely to be politically connected. In addition, it is investigated whether such probability increases at the time of recession (third chapter). The fourth chapter focuses only on one side of the revolving door. Specifically, it is asked whether highly regulated firms are more likely to either hire or appoint former politicians affiliated with a specific political party. Furthermore, it is asked whether firms belonging to the top regulated industries are more likely to either hire or appoint former politicians affiliated with a very strong political party at that time. In the fifth chapter, the market reaction at the announcement of a new political connection is analyzed. For this purpose, an event study is run by considering first the entire sample and then both sides of the revolving door separately, namely former politicians joining firms and former businessmen entering politics. Moreover, two subsamples are considered: the first one is related to firms among the top contractors and the second one is related to firms operating in the top regulated industries. Overall, the results show that industry-level regulation, political affiliation, and political environment matter.

Keywords political connections · highly regulated firms · highly regulated industries

M. Carboni, *The Financial Impact of Political Connections*,
DOI 10.1007/978-3-319-52776-5_6

The issue of political connections has been increasingly studied in recent years. Even if researchers show that political connections are relevant in countries characterized by high levels of corruption, more recent research demonstrates that they also impact strong legal environments. The last statement represents the basis for this book.

After providing a definition of connection, based on the movement between politics and business (the revolving door), and by exploiting a unique dataset for the time period 1999–2014, this book focuses on political connections in the United States. In particular, after a review of the main literature (second chapter), it is asked whether firms belonging to highly regulated industries are more likely to be politically connected (third chapter). The motivation for this work lies on the belief that industry-level regulation is a crucial issue across firms, since it is generally perceived as expensive and an impediment to business activities. For this reason, highly regulated firms should be more prone to look for political connections. Thanks to RegData (Al-Ubaydli and McLaughlin 2015), it is possible to identify the top regulated industries in the Unites States, and consequently analyze exhaustively whether firms operating in those industries tend to be connected with politicians. In addition, it is investigated whether such probability increases at the time of recession. The results show that highly regulated firms are actually more likely to be politically connected, regardless of recession. The existence of a correlation strengthens the findings of previous studies. However, such studies only take into account two or three regulated industries, without considering thoroughly all of them and without giving industry-level regulation the proper relevance in the establishment of political connections. The fourth chapter focuses only on one side of the revolving door, and in particular on the movement from politics to business. By using RegData again, it is asked whether highly regulated firms are more likely to either hire former politicians affiliated with a specific political party or appoint them as directors. The motivation for this research lies on the belief that Republicans are generally thought of as being pro-business. The results show that the most regulated firms are more likely to either hire former Republicans or appoint them as directors. Conversely, highly regulated firms are less likely to either hire former Democrats or appoint them as directors, confirming the initial assumption. A further question to answer is related to the "power" of a political party during a specific period of time. Therefore, it is asked whether firms belonging to the top regulated industries are more likely to either hire or appoint former politicians affiliated with a very strong political party.

The expectation is that the probability to either hire former Republicans or appoint them as directors increases if Republicans have the majority in the Congress and the President is also Republican. Vice versa, the strength of the political party should be less important or not important at all for the Democrats. The results confirm this intuition: highly regulated firms are more likely to either hire or appoint Republicans when they are "powerful", while the probability to either hire or appoint a former politician affiliated with the Democratic Party is higher if the firm does not belong to a top regulated industry, if Democrats do not have the majority in the Congress, and the President is not Democratic. It is possible to answer that question thanks to the time dimension of the dataset, which includes the years in which not only each political party has the majority in both the House of Representatives and the Senate but the President himself is affiliated with the ruling party.

In the fifth chapter, the market reaction at the announcement of a new political connection is analyzed. To this extent, an event study is run by considering first both sides of the revolving door, and then former politicians joining firms and former businessmen entering politics separately. Therefore, the hand-collected dataset is exploited one more time in order to identify political connections.

After looking at the full sample, the focus is on two subsamples, related to firms ranking among the top 100 contractors and firms operating in the top regulated industries. The results show that a significant evidence of positive reaction exists, but only when the two subgroups are considered and if former politicians join firms. In conclusion, the results of this chapter display that investors recognize the relevance of being politically connected if firms belong to highly regulated industries. The findings are therefore consistent with the view that industry-level regulation matters.

Appendix A

The sample consists of politicians of both US Legislative (the Senate and the House of Representatives) and Executive Branches (the President, the Vice President, the principal executives of the Executive Office of the President, the Cabinet), in office in the period January 2000–September 2014. The initial sample consists of 1,507 person-position combinations. A unique identification code is created and then associated with every politician. In addition, for each individual, information about political party, birthplace, birth date, gender, education (and in particular: name of the university, graduation year, academic discipline), work experience, family composition, religious affiliation, and military service is hand-collected.

Some politicians had a "business career" as founders, directors, and/or corporate executives, before or after entering politics. The focus is only on careers in listed firms, and these firms are identified as "politically connected".[1] Based on the author's specific definition of political connection, 131 politicians are politically connected. Because of the employed definition of political connection, such connections are entirely legal. Table A.1 provides a list of the sources.

In order to associate a code to firms, the SEC's EDGAR database is used. In this way, politically connected firms are linked to the Central Index Key (CIK). The filings provided by that database are used to further

M. Carboni, *The Financial Impact of Political Connections*,
DOI 10.1007/978-3-319-52776-5

Table A.1 List of the Main Sources to Identify Politicians and Political Connections

Biographical Directory of the United States Congress (http://bioguide.congress.gov/biosearch/biosearch.asp)
The White House (https://www.whitehouse.gov/)
Office of the Historian (https://history.state.gov/)
OpenCongress
Bipartisan Policy Center
Personal websites of politicians
Universities Websites
Corporate Websites
SEC's EDGAR Database
The Washington Post
The New York Times
The Wall Street Journal
The Huffington Post
Bloomberg
Forbes
Reuters
Washington Business Journal
Chicago Tribune
National Mortgage News
Arkansas Business
The Spokesman-Review
Biomass Magazine
PR Newswire
Business Wire
NYSE
Nasdaq
LinkedIn

Source: Author's own

obtain information on both former politicians joining firms and future politicians leaving firms to enter politics.

Finally, the dates of announcement of both corporate and political hiring/appointments and resignations are collected, by performing an extensive keyword search on LexisNexis. For example, in order to find the date of announcement related to a corporate appointment, are performed: *Name of the individual + join + name of the firm*, or *Name of the firm + appoint + name of the individual*, or *Name of the firm + elect + name of the individual.*

After identifying the connected politicians, politically connected firms, and the dates of the announcements of hiring/appointments and resignations, information on daily stock prices are collected. To this aim, it is convenient to identify politically connected firms also through the Ticker symbol, which enables to identify firms within databases that provide the daily stock prices. The Ticker symbols of S&P 500 components are also collected, so that, finally, the total number is equal to 720. Basically, that number includes the Ticker Symbols of S&P 500 components and politically connected firms out of the Index (as the Index is made of a part of the politically connected firms).

Next, two dummy variables are created within the database containing prices, namely *infirm* and *inpolitics*. These variables are equal to 1, respectively, when a former politician is announced to be either appointed as a director or hired as a corporate executive in a listed firm and when a former businessperson is announced to enter politics, and remain equal to 1 until the announcement of resignation. A further variable is created to indicate the number of former politicians in firms (*numberformerpoliticiansinfirm*) along with a variable indicating the number of former businesspeople in politics (*numberformerbusinesspinpolit*). To work in a homogeneous way, the 720 Ticker symbols are also used to download data on financial statements (balance sheets and income statements).

The final dataset consists of 2,135,437 observations[2] and 776 variables. It comprehends S&P 500 components and politically connected firms (both in and out of the Index). The dataset also contains a third group of companies, which are neither S&P 500 components nor politically connected firms. These companies are in the dataset simply because they have the same Ticker symbols of either politically connected firms or S&P 500 components.

Notes

1. Parent companies are selected. If politicians are connected with a non-listed firm having a parent company listed in the United States, the latter is selected and considered as politically connected.
2. Only listed firms with one share class traded on US stock exchanges are kept.

References

Akey, P. "Valuing changes in political networks: Evidence from campaign contributions to close congressional elections." *Review of Financial Studies* 28 (2015): 3188–3223.

Al-Ubaydli, O., & McLaughlin, P. A. "RegData: A numerical database on industry-specific regulations for all United States industries and federal regulations, 1997–2012." *Regulation & Governance* (2015). doi: 10.1111/rego.12107.

Amici, A., Fiordelisi, F., Masala, F., Ricci, O., & Sist, F. "Value creation in banking through strategic alliances and joint ventures." *Journal of Banking and Finance* 37(2013): 1386–1396.

Amore, M. D., & Bennedsen, M. "The value of local political connections in a low-corruption environment." *Journal of Financial Economics* 110(2013): 387–402.

Berman, J. "Wall Street and Washington share millions of dollars, lot of people." *The Huffington Post*, August 30, 2012. Accessed October 31, 2016, http://www.huffingtonpost.com/2012/08/30/wall-street-washington_n_1842517.html.

Blanes I Vidal, J., Draca, M., & Fons-Rosen, C. "Revolving door lobbyists." *American Economic Review* 102(2012): 3731–3748.

Boehmer, E., Musumeci, J., & Poulsen, A. "Event-study methodology under conditions of event-induced variance." *Journal of Financial Economics* 30 (1991): 253–272.

Boesler, M., & Kearns, J.. "'Revolving door' between fed and banks spins faster." *Bloomberg*, January 30, 2015. Accessed October 31, 2016. http://www.bloomberg.com/news/articles/2015-01-30/fed-s-revolving-door-spins-faster-as-banks-boost-hiring.

M. Carboni, *The Financial Impact of Political Connections*,
DOI 10.1007/978-3-319-52776-5

Borisov, A., Goldman, E., & Gupta, N. "The corporate value of (corrupt) lobbying." *Review of Financial Studies* 29(2015): 1039–1071.

Bunkanwanicha, P., & Wiwattanakatang, Y. "Big business owners in politics." *Review of Financial Studies* 22(2009): 2133–2168.

Carretta, A., Farina, V., Gon, A., & Parisi, A. "Politicians 'on board': Do political connections affect banking activities in Italy?." *European Management Review* 9(2012): 75–83.

Claessens, S., Feijen, E., & Laeven, L. "Political connections and preferential access to finance: The role of campaign contributions." *Journal of Financial Economics* 88(2008): 554–580.

Cooper, M. J., Gulen, H., & Ovtchinnikov, A. V. "Corporate political contributions and stock returns." *Journal of Finance* 65(2010): 687–724.

Creswell, J., & White, B.. "The guys from 'Government Sachs'." *The New York Times*, October 17, 2008. Accessed October 31, 2016. http://www.nytimes.com/2008/10/19/business/19gold.html.

Cummins, J. D., & Weiss, M. A. "Consolidation in the European insurance industry. Do mergers and acquisitions create value for shareholders?." *Brookings–Wharton Papers on Financial Services* (2004): 217–258.

Duchin, R., & Sosyura, D. "The politics of government investment." *Journal of Financial Economics* 106(2012): 24–48.

The Editorial Board. "Conflicts of interest at the F.D.A." *The New York Times*, April 13, 2015. Accessed October 31, 2016. http://www.nytimes.com/2015/04/13/opinion/conflicts-of-interest-at-the-fda.html.

Eggen, D., & Kindy, K.. "Three of every four oil and gas lobbyists worked for federal government." *The Washington Post*, July 22, 2010. Accessed October 31, 2016. http://www.washingtonpost.com/wp-dyn/content/article/2010/07/21/AR2010072106468.html.

Faccio, M. "Politically connected firms." *American Economic Review* 96(2006): 369–386.

Faccio, M., Masulis, R.W., & McConnell, J.J. "Political connections and corporate bailouts." *Journal of Finance* 61(2006): 2597–2635.

Fan, J.P.H., Wong, T. J., & Zhang, T. "Politically connected CEOs, corporate governance, and post-IPO performance of China's newly partially privatized firms." *Journal of Financial Economics* 84(2007): 330–357.

Ferguson, T., & Voth, H.-J. "Betting on Hitler – The value of political connections in Nazi Germany." *Quarterly Journal of Economics* 123(2008): 101–137.

Fisman, R. "Estimating the value of political connections." *American Economic Review* 91(2001): 1095–1102.

Goldman, E., Rocholl, J., & So, J. "Do politically connected boards affects firm value?." *Review of Financial Studies* 22(2009): 2331–2360.

Goldman, E., Rocholl, J., & So, J. "Politically Connected Board of Directors and the allocation of procurement contracts." *Review of Finance* 17(2013): 1617–1648.

"GOP Vs. Democrats: Who's best for America's economy?." *Forbes*, August 31, 2012. Accessed October 31, 2016. http://www.forbes.com/sites/investopedia/2012/08/31/gop-vs-democrats-whos-best-for-americas-economy/#1dcce5a13e80.

Gorodnichenko, Y., & Weber, M. "Are Sticky Prices Costly? Evidence from the Stock Market." (online appendix) *American Economic Review*, 106(2016): 165–199.

Harrington, S., & Shrider, D. "All events induce variance: Analyzing abnormal returns when effects vary across firms." *Journal of Financial and Quantitative Analysis* 42(2007): 229–256.

Jenkins, P. "'Revolving door' trend takes hold in Europe." *Financial Times*, July 29, 2016. Accessed October 31, 2016. https://www.ft.com/content/4fc3a7b4-5599-11e6-9664-e0bdc13c3bef.

Khwaja, A.I., & Mian, A. "Do lenders favor politically connected firms? Rent provision in an emerging financial market." *Quarterly Journal of Economics* 120(2005): 1371–1411.

Kim, C.F., Pantzalis, C., & Park, J. C. "Political geography and stock returns: The value and risk implications of proximity to political power." *Journal of Financial Economics* 106(2012): 196–228.

Kolari, J. W., & Pynnönen, S. "Event study testing with cross-sectional correlation of abnormal returns." *Review of Financial Studies* 23(2010): 3996–4025.

Lipton, E. "The revolving door: An annotated case study." *The New York Times*, February 2, 2014. Accessed October 31, 2016. http://www.nytimes.com/interactive/2014/02/02/us/politics/02revolving-door-documents.html.

McLaughlin, P.A., & Sherouse, O. "The Impact of Federal Regulation on the 50 States." 2016 ed. (Arlington, VA: Mercatus Center at George Mason University, 2016).

Mentz, M., & Schiereck, D. "Cross-border mergers and the cross-border effect: The case of the automotive supply industry." *Review of Managerial Science* 2 (2008): 199–218.

Mikkelson, W. H., & Partch, M. M. "Withdrawn security offerings." *Journal of Financial and Quantitative Analysis* 23(1988): 119–133.

Ovtchinnikov, A. V., & Pantaleoni, E. "Individual political contributions and firm performance." *Journal of Financial Economics* 105(2012): 367–392.

Slocum, T. "Chevron banks on profitable political agenda." *The Huffington Post*, May 26, 2011. Accessed October 31, 2016. http://www.huffingtonpost.com/tyson-slocum/chevron-banks-on-profitab_b_867408.html.

Tahoun, A. "The role of stock ownership by US members of Congress on the market for political favors." *Journal of Financial Economics* 111(2014): 86–110.

Index

M. Carboni, *The Financial Impact of Political Connections*,
DOI 10.1007/978-3-319-52776-5

Printed by Printforce, the Netherlands